From Moment to Meaning

The Art of Scholar-Practitioner Inquiry

Maria Piantanida
Marilyn J. Llewellyn
Patricia L. McMahon

Wisdom of Practice Series

Learning Moments Press
Pittsburgh, PA

From Moment to Meaning: The Art of Scholar-Practitioner Inquiry
Published by Learning Moments Press
Pittsburgh, PA 15139
Learningmomentspress.com

ISBN-13 978-1-7349594-0-6
BISAC Subject: Education/Research (EDU037000); Education/Philosophy,
Theory & Social Aspects (EDU 04000); Education/Essay (EDU042000)

Onix audience Code: 06 Professional & Scholarly

Book Layout
Mike Murray, pearhouse.com

To the countless dedicated Scholar-Practitioners
who work tirelessly as stewards of the profession.

Table of Contents

List of Scenarios

Prologue

In the spring of 2020, the COVID-19 virus swept across the globe, disrupting ordinary life in unprecedented ways. Hot spots in the United States stressed the health care system to its limits. Businesses shuttered their doors and the economy ground to a halt. Schools across the country closed, sending millions of children home to learn from on-line classes prepared by hundreds of thousands of teachers. As the pandemic crested, politicians, media pundits, and knowledgeable experts began to speculate about when life could get back to normal. Although they differed on when and how to reopen the country, they all agreed that no one could predict exactly what the "new normal" would look like. Writing in what Joshua Cooper Ramo calls "the age of the unthinkable," we ponder the question, "What might constitute the new normal of education in a post-pandemic world?"

Ramo contends that old ways of thinking do not serve us well in an increasingly complex world where the whole is more than the sum of the parts and the parts interact to produce unforeseen effects. Trying to impose some ideally imagined order on complex and dynamic global systems is futile and, in fact, blinds us to possibilities that seem unthinkable. Ramo's field of international affairs, for example, is blinded by outdated views of power, war, and national security. A few men flying planes into iconic symbols of U.S. economic and military power was unthinkable. Consequently, we were unprepared to defend against a terrorist attack. Ramo calls for new ways of thinking to provide what he calls *deep security*. "Instead of starting with a view of how we want the world to be and then jamming that view into place, we start more reasonably with a picture of how the world is."[1] If we borrow from Ramo's concept of deep security, what new ways of thinking might lead to a "new normal" of educational systems founded on a principle of *deep learning*? Educators Linda Darling Hammer and

---

1 Joshua Cooper Ramo, *The Age of the Unthinkable: Why the New World Disorder Constantly Surprises Us* (New York: Back Bay Books, 2009), 108.

Jeannie Oakes express a similar view in *Preparing Teachers for Deeper Learning*, a book which

> ...answers an urgent call for teachers who educate children from diverse backgrounds to meet the demands of a changing world. In today's knowledge economy, teachers must prioritize problem-solving ability, adaptability, critical thinking, and the development of interpersonal and collaborative skills over rote memorization and the passive transmission of knowledge. Authors Linda Darling-Hammond and Jeannie Oakes and their colleagues examine what this means for teacher preparation and showcase the work of programs that are educating for deeper learning, equity, and social justice.[2]

For two decades, politicians, billionaire philanthropists, and politically connected educators have been jamming their views of education onto our public education system. Diane Ravitch calls these individuals "disrupters," asserting that their policies and strategies are anything but genuine reform.[3] Nassim Nicholas Taleb would call these proponents of "educational reform" "fragilistas," individuals "who make you engage in policies and actions, all artificial in which *the benefits are small and visible, and the side effects potentially severe and invisible.*"[4] (Italics in the original) Taleb contends:

> A complex system, contrary to what people believe, does not require complicated systems and regulations and intricate policies. The simpler, the better. Complications lead to multiplicative chains

---

2   Linda Darling Hammond and Jeannie Oakes, *Preparing Teachers for Deeper Learning* (San Francisco: John Wiley & Sons, 2005).

3   Diane Ravitch, *Slaying Goliath: Passionate Resistance to Privatization and the Fight to Save America's Public Schools* (New York: Alfred A. Knopf, 2020).

4   Nassim Nicholas Taleb, *Antifragile: Things that Gain from Disorder* (New York: Random House, 2012), 10.

> of unanticipated effects. Because of opacity, an intervention leads to unforeseen consequences, followed by apologies about the "unforeseen" aspect of the consequences, then to another intervention to correct the secondary effects, leading to an explosive series of branching "unforeseen" responses, each one worse than the preceding one. [5]

Old ways of thinking about systemic educational reform provide a perfect example of this point. *No Child Left Behind* followed by *Race to the Top* followed by the *Every Student Succeeds Act* imposed standardized accountability measures that resulted in "unforeseen" consequences that Ravitch describes in heart-breaking detail. As the toll on educators became unbearable:

> Many teachers decided they could no longer remain in their chosen profession because a draconian standards-and-testing regime mandated by federal law stole weeks, sometimes months, from classroom instruction, distorted the goals of education, and made it impossible for them to teach with autonomy, passion, and creativity.[6]

Ironically, when the COVID-19 pandemic forced school closings, teachers were suddenly freed from this oppressive oversight. The attention of the would-be reformers turned to our collapsing medical and economic systems. Left on their own, educators needed flexibility, adaptability, and creativity to respond in this "unthinkable" world of nation-wide distance learning. Both Ramo and Taleb contend these qualities are inherent in healthy, resilient, organically evolving systems. The post-pandemic challenge for educators is shaping a "new normal" of educational systems to assure autonomy, flexibility, adaptability, and creativity. Meeting this challenge calls for deep learning—the type of

---

5 Taleb, 11.
6 Ravitch, 3-4

learning at the heart of Scholar-Practitioner Inquiry. We write this book with the hope of encouraging those in all types of educational roles and settings to cultivate a Scholar-Practitioner mindset conducive to Scholar-Practitioner Inquiry.

Preface

PURPOSE OF THE BOOK

This book begins with the premise that "Scholar-Practitioner" is a distinctive professional mindset. In our book, *On Being a Scholar-Practitioner: Practical Wisdom in Action*, we describe six qualities embodied in this mindset: pedagogical wisdom, theoretical understanding, contextual literacy, ethical stewardship, metacognitive reflection, and aesthetic imagination. Together, these qualities take practitioners beyond the skillful application of methods and techniques to a stance of inquiry. The purpose of Scholar-Practitioner Inquiry is to cultivate these qualities, thereby enhancing the flexibility, adaptability, and creativity with which educators respond to the daily demands of their work. The twofold purpose of this book is to elaborate on the nature of Scholar-Practitioner Inquiry and to provide a framework to help educators embrace this stance of inquiry.

Organization of the Book

The book is divided into two sections. The chapters in *Section 1—Cultivating a Mindset for Scholar-Practitioner Inquiry* address the first purpose of the book. We begin by considering features that distinguish contextualized studies of practice from controlled scientific studies. Following this, we turn to the issues of method and then to the nature of evidence in Scholar-Practitioner Inquiry. This section concludes with a discussion of writing conventions that contribute to the conceptual integrity and coherence of Scholar-Practitioner Inquiries. *Section 2—Developing My Scholar-Practitioner Inquiry Profile* provides a framework for examining contexts of practice, professional concerns, and intellectual background that shape the sensibilities practitioners bring to their scholarship. Throughout the book we include *Scenarios* to illustrate points we are raising.

Each chapter in Section 2 has the same format. It begins with a brief explanation of the purpose of the chapter followed by a set of *Reflective Prompts*. As you read through these, make notes about ideas that come to mind. Early on, treat this as a brainstorming session where you want to record as many ideas as you can. As you continue to work on your *Profile*, you can begin to refine the ideas. Each chapter concludes with a *Reflective Interlude* which encourages you to think about connections among the ideas in various chapters.

Audience for the Book

The ideas presented in this book have emerged from our work with graduate and doctoral students enrolled in formal academic programs that required completion of a thesis, dissertation, or other form of capstone project. Therefore, the ideas presented are likely to be most relevant to readers who are engaged in formal, academic inquiry projects.

It is our hope, however, that the ideas may also appeal to practitioners who long for an intellectual life beyond the demands of daily practice. This intellectual longing may lie dormant under the incessant pressures of teaching or administration. Nevertheless, it points to an inclination for inquiry that can be nurtured through thoughtful reflection. The deep learning associated with Scholar-Practitioner Inquiry can better position all practitioners to advocate for vibrant educational systems that prepare students to thrive in a complex, dynamic, and changing world.

How to Use the Book

Understanding the nature of Scholar-Practitioner Inquiry and developing a Scholar-Practitioner Inquiry Profile are not linear processes. Both entail visiting and revisiting the ideas of others as well as thinking and rethinking your own ideas. This is an iterative process that slowly brings greater clarity and focus to Scholar-Practitioner Inquiries. You may want to read through the entire book to get a general feel for information provided. After that, we encourage you to skip around to the chapters that are most relevant at any particular time. Cross-references to chapters and scenarios are embedded throughout the text to facilitate the movement among various parts of the book.

Throughout the book you will encounter tips that may seem to state the obvious. Too often, however, we and others have lost sight of the obvious when we were deeply immersed in an inquiry.

 Create one or more computer files where you can continually update your thinking. In our own work, we learned the hard way that old, seemingly irrelevant, ideas shouldn't be deleted. Inevitably we found ourselves sifting through our trash files to find a tidbit of thinking that suddenly became very important. So, along with your most current version of your *Profile*, keep an archive of previous versions.

One final note relates to the writing style of the book. In places, we are dealing with some pretty weighty ideas. Even so, we strive for a conversational tone, as though we are sitting with a cup of coffee (or glass of wine) and talking about your questions and concerns. If you would like to engage in an even more focused conversation, please visit scholarpractitionernexus.com and submit a post in the *Share Your Thoughts--Blog* section of the website. We would love to engender some lively exchanges among those who are undertaking Scholar-Practitioner Inquiries.

SECTION 1

Cultivating a Mindset for Scholar-Practitioner Inquiry

"In the varied topography of professional practice, there is a high hard ground where practitioners can make effective use of research-based theory and technique, and there is a swampy lowland where situations are confusing 'messes' incapable of technical solution. The difficulty is that the problems of the high ground, however great their technical interest, are often relatively unimportant to clients or to the larger society, while in the swamp are the problems of greatest human concern."

– Donald A. Schon
The Reflective Practitioner

"I believe in standardizing automobiles. I do not believe in standardizing human beings. Standardization is a great peril which threatens American culture..."

– Albert Einstein

CHAPTER 1

On the Nature of Scholar-Practitioner Inquiry

A Brief Introduction to Scholar-Practitioner Inquiry

The overarching aim of educational research is to improve education. Under this broad purpose are multiple paths of inquiry. Somewhat arbitrarily (and at the risk of oversimplification), we characterize one of these pathways as "scientific research" and the other as "Scholar-Practitioner Inquiry." [1]

Those following the path of scientific research tend to work in academic settings, conducting large scale studies, funded by government or philanthropic grants. Generally, their research efforts are guided by the assumptions and procedures of scientific research. This research aims for objectivity and seeks causal relationships among factors that, statistically speaking, have a high probability of holding true across most, if not all, educational contexts. This form of educational research has its roots in the behaviorism, standardization, and quantitative measurement movements of the early 20th century. Today's efforts to demonstrate the efficacy of "best practices" and

---

1 Our intent in using the descriptors "scientific research" and "Scholar-Practitioner Inquiry" is not to offer a precise definition of either. Rather, we want to help beginning scholar-practitioners sort through what it means to engage in a study of their practice. Time and time again, we meet masters and doctoral students who approach their thesis or dissertation with vaguely formed notions of "scientific" research. They struggle with the question, "If it isn't science, then what is it?" Of course, volumes have been written on the nature of science, and those engaged in such deliberations have moved beyond the precepts of Newtonian physics to new ways of conceptualizing scientific research. However, students often use the idea of "scientific research" as a foil for their thinking. For this reason we find it useful to explore ways in which Scholar-Practitioner Inquiry can be rigorous even if it does not conform to several key principles commonly associated with the scientific process.

to measure educational performance through standardized testing are legacies of this behavioral-standardization-quantitative research tradition. Throughout the book, we refer to those engaged in this form of inquiry as "scientific educational researchers."

As the descriptor "Scholar-Practitioner Inquiry" connotes, those following this path tend to work within the settings of educational practice. Rather than engaging in large-scale, funded projects, they tend to engage in deep learning to heighten their capacity for pedagogical wisdom, theoretic understanding, contextual literacy, ethical stewardship, metacognitive reflection, and/or aesthetic imagination. Typically, Scholar-Practitioner Inquiries are situated within contexts where educators carry out their day-to-day responsibilities. Rather than generating generalizable knowledge, they examine problematic issues, seeking insights into the nuances of educational practice. This form of inquiry has its roots in the interpretive traditions of the arts and humanities. This is the reason the title of the book refers to the *art* of "Scholar-Practitioner Inquiry."

Although interpretation plays an important role in both scientific and interpretive research, interpretation in Scholar-Practitioner Inquiry cannot claim to be objective. Scholar-practitioners as inquirers are not dispassionate observers. They are active participants, indeed agents, in the questions under study. Interpretation in this sense entails discernment and judgment. Discernment is a capacity to see the salient features of practice. Judgment involves describing those salient features and making explicit the values upon which judgments are made. Our capacity to see and judge is shaped by who we are; what we believe; what we value; what we know; what we hope to accomplish. Obviously, as Scholar-Practitioners, we cannot separate ourselves from these subjective aspects of who we are. But, through study—through inquiry—we can better understand the lenses through which we see and make judgments. The outcome of such Scholar-Practitioner Inquiry is what Barry Schwartz and Kenneth Sharpe call practical wisdom.

Practical wisdom entails a capacity to figure out "…the right way to do the right thing in a particular circumstance, with a particular person, at a particular time."[2] Often, in the hectic pace of daily practice, seeing and responding take place in an instant. When our knowledge, instincts,

---

2   Barry Schwartz and Kenneth Sharpe, *Practical Wisdom: The Right Way to Do the Right Thing* (New York: Riverhead Books, 2010), 5-6.

interpretations, judgments, and responses lead to desired and desirable outcomes, that instant of action may quickly recede from memory. When the outcome goes awry, that moment may linger, causing us to wonder: What went wrong? What did I miss? What could I have done differently? Why wasn't I wise enough to see that coming? What didn't I understand? These troubling moments are often the starting point for a Scholar-Practitioner Inquiry.

From Moment to Inquiry

Acknowledging a troubling moment and wanting to learn from it set Scholar-Practitioners on a path of inquiry. An initial Exploratory Phase entails a search to find out if others have encountered a similar troubling situation and, if so, what have they said about it. By talking informally with colleagues and consulting other resources (e.g., books, articles, podcasts), Scholar-Practitioners begin to tease out the nature of trouble embedded in the moment. For example, the trouble might be related to:

- Issues—vital, unsettled, typically multifaceted, matters, or
- Problematics—circumstances in which complex factors prevent clear, definitive solutions,[3] or
- Dilemmas—choices between two or more courses of action, each of which has the potential for positive and negative consequences.

These forms of trouble are what Schon means by the "swampy lowlands" of messy practice and what David Cohen calls "predicaments."[4] These troubles do not lend themselves to the type of

---

3 In many forms of research, it is typical to include a "statement of the problem," meaning the problem to be studied. In the world of practice, the term "problem" often connotes a disruption in a normal and desirable state of affairs, and problem-solving research efforts seek pragmatic action to ameliorate or eradicate a problem. The focus on immediate problem solution may or may not be indicative of a scholarly mindset. For this reason, we prefer to use the concept of problematics and encourage Scholar-Practitioners to state an "intent of the study" or "an inquiry question to be investigated."

4 David K. Cohen, *Teaching and Its Predicaments* (Cambridge, MA: Harvard University Press, 2011).

objective knowledge generated through scientific research. They often entail difficult balancing among competing needs, interests, and values. (Scenarios 1.1, 1.2 and 1.3 provide examples of troubling moments.)

As Scholar-Practitioners gain preliminary insight into the underlying nature of the trouble that is bothering them, they are also encountering information that can lead to at least three major outcomes of the Exploratory Phase. In one case, Scholar-Practitioners might locate information that provides sufficient understanding that they feel no need for additional study. The source of their troubling moment has been clarified and the past event has been put to rest. The new insight engenders a sense of greater confidence about recognizing and responding to similar events in the future. This is an important outcome and one that might be most feasible for educators who are not enrolled in formal academic programs.

A second potential outcome entails a recognized need for further study. Scholar-Practitioners may encounter a wealth of information related to their troubling moment. Suddenly they realize they've based their practice on a fairly limited storehouse of knowledge. This is not an uncommon situation for beginning educational practitioners including teachers, administrators, and those providing supportive services (e.g., speech or occupational therapy) whose preservice education could provide only a modicum of all the knowledge needed for competent and wise practice.

When confronted by the limits of their knowledge, Scholar-Practitioners may choose to attend workshops, watch YouTube videos, listen to podcasts, and read reference materials that provide deeper insight into the troubling issue. Some choose to pursue graduate education. Through the course of their studies, they may realize they need time to digest a newly discovered treasure trove of knowledge. For example, Alexandra entered a Master's program wanting to know how to use rewards and punishments more effectively for classroom management. Early in the Exploratory Phase, she heard a presentation by Alfie Kohn, a vehement critic of rewards and punishments (euphemistically called "consequences"). This presentation opened the door to an unfamiliar body of literature about pedagogical authority, motivation, and learning. Through a Master's level inquiry, she explored this wealth of scholarly material and gained a deeper, more nuanced understanding of her pedagogy. Robert Nash[5] characterized this type of inquiry as a scholarly personal narrative. From our perspective, this is among the more useful forms of Master's level Scholar-Practitioner Inquiry.

A third potential outcome of the Exploratory Phase is particularly relevant to those enrolled in doctoral programs. By talking informally with others and exploring existing literature, Scholar-Practitioners conclude that a deeper understanding of their troubling moment is warranted—not just for themselves, but for others who are struggling with the same issue, problematic, dilemma, or predicament. This outcome positions Scholar-Practitioners to propose a study for their dissertation.

From Exploration to Inquiry Proposal

Developing a dissertation proposal entails crafting a response to three key questions:

- What am I going to study?
- Why is such a study worthwhile?
- How will I conduct my study?

To address the first two questions, a more systematic reading of literature will probably be necessary. For example, if Alexandra were enrolled in a doctoral program, she might need to read more extensively about pedagogical authority, motivation, classroom management, and learning. Through this reading she would see several different study possibilities. To write her proposal, she would need to decide, "This is what I am going to study; this is the intent of my study." Based on her reading, she would also be prepared to explain why her study would be worthwhile. She would have identified more clearly who is talking about the issue of classroom management, pedagogical authority, motivation, and learning. She would see what type of contribution her study could make to the on-going conversations about these issues.

---

5   Robert Nash, *Liberating Scholarly Writing: The Power of Personal Narrative* (New York: College Teachers Press, 2004).

The time involved in doing the reading necessary to craft a solid statement of intent and rationale for a dissertation is the reason we say it is never too early to begin exploring troubling moments of practice. Using course work to explore various bodies of knowledge can spread the necessary reading over several semesters, moving you more slowly and surely to the question you are passionate about studying.

The question of "How I will conduct my study" takes us full circle to the difference between scientific research and interpretive Scholar-Practitioner Inquiry and two different conceptions of "method."

> Method can be characterized in at least two ways. The most commonly encountered meaning is *method as procedures or techniques*. In this case the term invokes the kinds of "how-to-do-it" discussions long found in introductory textbooks on quantitative inquiry, and more recently, in a number of basic textbooks on qualitative inquiry...The second characterization of method is as *"logic-of-justification"*...The focus here is not on techniques but on the elaboration of logical issues and, ultimately, on the justifications that inform practice...This conceptualization involves such basic questions as, What is the nature of social and educational reality? What is the relationship of the investigator to what is investigated? And How is truth to be defined?[6] (italics added)

Method in the sense of how-to procedures is more typical of scientific research. When science was the default paradigm for thinking about educational research, the underlying assumptions about the nature of educational reality and truth were so pervasive the logics of a

---

6   John K. Smith, and Lous Heshusius, "Closing Down the Conversation: The End of the Quantitative-Qualitative Debate among Educational Inquirers," *Educational Researcher* (January 1986): 8.

study did not have to be explicitly stated. The logics were understood by researchers and those who would judge their work.

The emergence of Scholar-Practitioner Inquiry presented a conundrum, because scientific assumptions about method did not seem suited to interpretive studies. For example, consider the following anecdote:

> A doctoral student from China told her advisor she wanted to study the experience of Chinese students when they came to the United States. "But you can't study that," her advisor said. "You're a Chinese woman who came here to study. You couldn't be objective."

While it is true she couldn't be objective, it is not true that she couldn't study the issue. Her advisor's pronouncement rested on an assumption about "objectivity" as a *sine qua non* of research. Based on assumptions of interpretive inquiry, her study could be quite feasible. In fact, her experience of adjusting to life in the Unites States might be the very thing that allows her to generate important insights into this experience.[7]

Because multiple paths for educational research co-exist, Scholar-Practitioners need to clarify which path they are following. Those who follow the path of interpretive, Scholar-Practitioner Inquiry cannot assume that others will understand the logics that underpin their "method." For this reason, we prefer to think of method as "logic-of-justification." Developing a logic-of-justification involves describing both the procedures of the study and the reason for those procedures. We elaborate on this point in the following chapter.

---

7 For a compelling example of such a "subjective" inquiry, see Suki Kim, *Without You, There is No Us: Undercover among the Sons of North Korea's Elite* (New York: Penguin Random House, 2014). Kim was born in South Korea but grew up in the United States. She spent two semesters teaching English in a school run by missionaries in North Korea. She entered into this experience with the intention of writing a book and drew upon her skills as an investigative journalist to keep detailed notes upon which she based *Without You, There is No Us*. In part, her desire to carry out this project stemmed from lifelong questions about her sense of identity and the pain caused to so many Korean families by the division of their country. Had she been a doctoral student talking with the advisor in this anecdote, she would have been told, "You can't do that study. You couldn't be objective."

....
SCENARIO 1.1
DESCRIBING A MOMENT OF PRACTICE

A Focus on a Troubling Role

My interest in the professional practice of hospital education began in the spring of 1978 when I accepted the position of "Resident of Education" at a large, urban, teaching hospital. Patterned after the model of the medical residency, the position had been established to give doctoral level students in the field of education an intensive, practice-oriented learning experience. The need for such an educational opportunity had been perceived by several of the hospital's administrators who believed that educators could more effectively apply their knowledge and skills if they understood the hospital environment.

My decision to accept the Resident position was based on several considerations. Having recently completed my doctoral course work, I was eager to use what I had been learning in an organizational setting. In addition, the next step in my educational program was my dissertation research. The Resident position, clearly established for someone working in a "student" capacity, seemed to offer an ideal opportunity to pursue my research project. Previous medically related work experience and a long standing affinity for health care made hospital education a logical choice for me.

The length of the Residency had been set at eight months, and the hospital had made no commitment to employ me on a permanent basis beyond that time. Therefore, my intention upon entering the position was to focus a research question and use my time in the Residency to complete my doctoral research. In making these plans, I was essentially saying, "Not only am I interested in practicing education in a hospital setting, I am also interested in seriously researching the nature of that practice."

Almost as soon as I walked through the doors of the hospital, my neatly formulated plans began to disintegrate. Everything was so new and confusing. I was so inundated with information that my most demanding task was trying to get and keep my bearings. During this time, a number of people were very willing to tell me what I should be doing and how I should be doing it. I might have found some comfort in their well-meant advice except for two factors. First, the advice from one source often was in direct contradiction with the advice from other sources. Second, a great deal of the proffered advice was inconsistent with much of what I knew and believed about adult education. For many months I felt as though I were mired in a quicksand of confusion with no firm ground upon which to stand and act. When, at the end of the eight-month Residency, I was offered a permanent staff position, I concluded that I must have been doing something right—but what, I was not sure. Nevertheless, I was pleased, for it gave me an opportunity to continue practicing and learning about education in hospitals.

AFTER WORD

Shortly after completing my dissertation, I had hoped to refashion it into a publishable book. At the time, I was trying to bridge between two discourse communities—hospital educators who tended to focus narrowly on the details of practice and educators in the professions who valued research. As part of this bridging effort, I had served as guest editor for a special, research-focused issue of a journal published by an association of hospital educators. One of the invited authors was an educator who was versed in qualitative as well as quantitative research. When I turned to this senior researcher for some publication advice, he summarily dismissed my work with a terse, "This isn't theoretical." I wish I had been able to respond with a perspective on research offered by some of the most respected scholars in the field of curriculum:

> The point of contemporary curriculum research is to stimulate self-reflection, self-understanding, and social change. Simply put, practical or theoretical research is intended as much to provoke questions as it is to answer questions. As Joe Kincheloe suggests:

"Theorizing is a tentative process of reflection about one's experience for the purpose of becoming an author of that experience." [8]

At the time, I didn't fully understand the importance of discourse communities or learning how to talk with others whose assumptions about research fell within the scientific tradition. This troubling moment was among several that fueled my commitment to help others understand the nature of interpretive inquiry.

Ironically enough, a number of years after my abbreviated contact with the senior researcher, he published a highly personal account of his father's death, which was anything but theoretical.

---

8   William F. Pinar, William M. Reynolds, Patrick Slattery, and Peter M. Taubman, *Understanding Curriculum* (New York: Peter Lang, 1995) 56-57.

SCENARIO 1.2
DESCRIBING A MOMENT OF PRACTICE

A Focus on Pedagogical Trouble

COMMENTARY

Jerome Bruner talks about "trouble" as the engine that drives narrative. Narratives often begin—not with these specific words—but with the idea that "I was walking along minding my own business, when all of a sudden..." Encountering the unexpected startles the narrator out of a state of equilibrium. The narrative story then recounts how the narrator responded in an effort to resolve the precipitating trouble.

Patricia L. McMahon (Pat) works within the narrative tradition. In this Scenario she describes a startling moment that precipitated her inquiry. As you read this anecdote, notice how Pat moves from describing the situational details (who, when, where) to what was troubling her. Notice how she moves from her own situation to the broader context of her life as a teacher and her overarching pedagogical concern. In the final paragraph, she begins to bridge into a broader community that might share her concern—i.e., teachers of college composition and teachers who want to engage students more effectively in classroom life. It would be misleading to imply that Pat wrote this description off the top of her head. Indeed, she spent quite a bit of time probing the source of her uneasiness about her pedagogy. But the seed for her study was embedded in an encounter that could easily have been dismissed or forgotten in the hectic pace of practice. (*Scenario 4.2* provides additional details of Pat's final study.)

I was standing in the hallway outside my community college classroom, listening to one of my former students speak to me about his education. He had enrolled in one of my composition courses at the beginning of his academic career. A little over two years later, he was about to graduate. I expected his mood to be as bright as the sunshine that had found its way through the open front doors and now lit the space outside my classroom. But this was not the case. This student was not joyful; he was concerned.

"Shouldn't I be able to remember something that I learned? Shouldn't I have a feeling of accomplishing something?" he wondered aloud. When I asked if he could help me understand what he meant, he told me that he had been thinking about it for quite a while and could honestly say that he was unable to recall one piece of information he had learned. Hoping for a different way to represent his academic work, I suggested that maybe trying to recall pieces of information was not as important as understanding major concepts from the subjects he had studied or knowing how scholars in the various content areas come to make knowledge. "Maybe," I offered, "you know more than you realize."

It is difficult to forget how sad he became. He shook his head no and said, "Concepts? If that's what the purpose was, why have I just spent years of my life memorizing information, taking tests to show how much I can memorize, and forgetting every bit of information by the end of the exam?"

I could not respond. I knew he was right. How could he possibly regard the graduation ceremony as a meaningful experience when, for him, there had been no meaning to his entire educational experience?

My former student's state of mind and heart was infectious. It tapped into my own sadness, that of a teacher who for some time had been unsatisfied with her own ability to create a classroom environment that excited both students and me. I had tried varying my presentations in a number of ways, but increasingly I left the classroom right behind two uninvited visitors, Exhaustion and Guilt.

As painful as it was to reflect on my pedagogy, I did, relentlessly, and in the process I discovered an interesting correlation. My exhaustion was directly related to my guilt. The more exhausted I was by the end of a class, the more I was consumed by guilt. At this point I knew two things: I did not want my energy totally spent by the end of every day, nor did I want to pretend for one more day that my exhaustion did not signify anything profound. What it meant quite simply was that while I was immersed in the learning events of my curriculum, my students were merely observing. In fact, they embraced passivity whole-heartedly, I realized, because I was not asking them to do much more than just that—observe.

Over the years of teaching, I had abandoned the skills-based approach to writing as well as teaching rhetorical modes. Although I had made some progress in pursuing a pedagogy that emphasized the act of composing as a process, I still needed to involve my students more rigorously—not only in their own writing process, but also in the life of the class. I wanted some company in the classroom, but as long as I was perceived as the only person with questions, answers, and opinions, I would continue to feel isolated. The solution to my problem, I believed, lay in giving my students more responsibility for their writing and for the learning experience itself.

....
SCENARIO 1.3
DESCRIBING A TROUBLING
MOMENT OF PRACTICE

A Focus on an Educational Policy

COMMENTARY
....

This example comes from Micheline Stabile's dissertation and offers an example of just how long troubling moments can last and their power to shape a lifetime of professional practice and advocacy. (It also offers an interesting glimpse of how second grade "used to be" in "the olden days.") Notice, in particular, how Micheline bridges between her past role as second grade teacher to her current role as a school administrator with responsibilities for special education within her large urban school district. This is a nice example of how multiple roles and settings shape the lenses through which a current dilemma is viewed. We return to Micheline's dissertation in Scenario 4.3.

One of the most traumatic events of my professional career was the "failing" of one of my young second-grade students in my first year of teaching. I never realized how pivotal this event was until more than twenty-five years later when I wrote a narrative called:

For Timmy

On the first day of school we searched for a seat large enough to accommodate him...the good natured, orange haired, lumbering farm boy dressed in worn clothes handed down again and again from his seven older brothers and sisters. No stranger to this room, he escorted his new teacher into the world of second grade.

That year the young students in this small rural school under the guidance of their enthusiastic first year teacher explored the exciting challenges of the second grade curriculum. We laughed our way through *Mrs. Piggy Wiggle*, cried our way through *Charlotte's Web*, and struggled to "Think and Do" our way through endless phonics rules, thinly disguised as stories via Dick and Jane.

The challenges of second grade were renowned: cursive writing, "borrowing and carrying," telling time, and singing a round. Each second grade success was considered a triumph and was cherished by the young changelings as verification of their growth...a sign of growth just as exciting and true as the new "second" teeth just beginning to emerge, filling the empty spaces that were the last vestiges of babyhood.

Timmy's ever present smile was hauntingly different from the others. The bright blue of his eyes was different also, the childhood sparkle progressively dulled by a vacancy as he struggled persistently and vainly to "keep up" with the other "yellow birds." Tests revealed "marginal ability" and not much else in the way of hope or help for either student or his novice teacher.

On the last day of that memorable school year emotional good-byes accompanied report cards. Timmy's tears were hauntingly different, etched in my memory as persistent as his smile had once been.

Timmy and I...each a teacher and each a student.
One moved on to shape a new future.
One stayed behind to spend year another year
in the second grade class of
A small rural school....

Who Failed?

Thus I discovered that my professional path and studies in the field of education have been largely guided by my initial experiences within the profession as an elementary school teacher. When I reflect upon what brought me to this study of educational inclusion, I find that I must travel back to this beginning point. For in recalling my first year of teaching, I realize that from the start I became challenged by the group of students that was resistant to the typical traditional instructional practices and structures of our educational system.

Through the years I came to think of these students who fail within the system, as those whom the *system* fails, and to view the various labels created to classify "their" dysfunction as social constructions of questionable educational relevance. My interest in gaining an understanding of how our educational system might better serve the needs of this group of "unsuccessful" students has led me to seek and to advocate for alternative pedagogical approaches and policies throughout my professional lifetime. And so, it is all the more puzzling to me that when the educational inclusion movement swept into my professional world I was taken totally off guard, not by the addition of yet another reform initiative, but rather by my reaction to it. As a woman who personally stands to benefit from inclusion as a societal value and as a professional who considers herself to be an advocate for students, I was confused by my own immediate ambivalence to the movement, my concern about what it might mean for students, and my fear of the strong political rhetoric that characterized its onset.

CHAPTER 2

Method as
Logic-of-Justification

Our distinction between scientific research and Scholar-Practitioner Inquiry provides a shorthand reference for three interconnected clusters of assumptions (Figure 2.1):

- Axiological Assumptions focus on what form(s) of knowledge are valued.

- Ontological Assumptions focus on the nature of reality and our relationship to reality.

- Epistemological Assumptions focus on the nature of knowledge and the methods by which knowledge is generated.

Taken together, these assumptions constitute the mindset or world view that shapes the logics (methods) of a study.

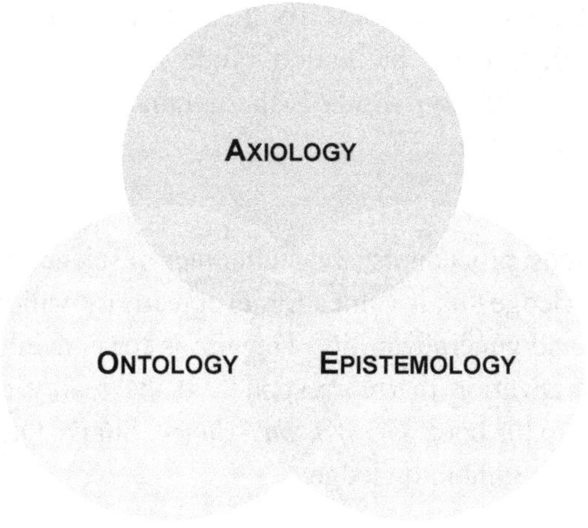

Figure 2.1 – World View

As mentioned in Chapter 1, one path of educational research follows the traditions of science. Social scientist, Bent Flyvbjerg provides a succinct distillation of the epistemological, ontological, and axiological assumptions that underpin science and its quest for "ideal theory":

> It [ideal theory] must be *explicit* because a theory is to be laid out so clearly, in such detail, and so completely that it can be understood by any reasoning being; a theory may not stand or fall on interpretation or intuition. Second, a theory must be *universal* in that it must apply in all places and all times. Third, a theory must be *abstract* in that it must not require the reference to concrete examples...A theory must also be *discrete*, that is, formulated only with the aid of context-independent elements, which do not refer to human interests, traditions, institutions, etc. And it must be *systematic*, that is, it must constitute a whole, in which context-independent elements (properties, facts) are related to each other by rules or laws... Finally, it must be *complete* and *predictive*. The way a theory accounts for the domain it covers must be comprehensive in the sense that it specifies the range of variation in the elements, which affect the domain, and the theory must specify their effects. This makes possible precise prediction. Today, it is especially this last criterion which is the hallmark of epistemic sciences.[1]

The methods, procedures, and techniques of science are designed to generate knowledge that is valued for its objectivity, validity, reliability, replicability, and generalizability. The aim is for convergence upon an abstract generalization that corresponds to the reality of an external phenomenon. In his book *The War on Science*, Shawn Otto sums up the process of converging knowledge:

---

1   Bent Flyvbjerg, *Making Social Science Matter: Why Social Inquiry Fails and How It Can Succeed Again*, trans. Steven Sampson (New York: Cambridge University Press, 2001), 38-39.

The [scientific] method is fallible, since our senses and our logical processes are easily influenced by our assumptions and wishes, and so they often mislead us. But over time the *method* tends to catch those errors and correct them via peer review and replication [of studies]. Thus, bit by careful, painstaking bit, we build a literature of what we know, as distinct from our beliefs and our opinions...[2] (italics added)

Often medical research is held up as the exemplar of ideal scientific research.[3] For decades, educational researchers emulated the medical model by looking for interventions that could ameliorate deficiencies in learning or correct dysfunctional organizational systems. Time and time again, however, the results of this research fell short of the validity, reliability, generalizability, and probabilistic certainty of ideal scientific theory.

The elusiveness of scientifically validated educational knowledge gave rise to the growing interest in interpretive inquiry, and more recently to Scholar-Practitioner Inquiry as a form of doctoral research. Shawn Otto's closing statement points to the conundrum faced by Scholar-Practitioners whose assumptions are embedded in the traditions of the arts and humanities. To the example of the Chinese student, we add the anecdotes in *Scenarios 2.1 and 2.2.*

Is it true that there is no such thing as qualitative (read interpretive) research as the physician in *Scenario 2.1* claims? Are we left, as Shawn

---

2   Shawn Lawrence Otto, *The War on Science: Who's Making It; Why It Matters; What We Can Do about It.* (Minneapolis: Milkweed Editions, 2016), 47.
3   The much touted certainty of medical knowledge may reside more in the hopes of anxious laypersons than in studies that rarely yield 100% certainty that a given treatment will be effective. Nevertheless, medical research continues to serve as a beacon for research within the scientific tradition of Newtonian physics. More recent conceptions of research in many fields (including the basic sciences) acknowledge that getting to the "reality" of complex systems goes beyond what scientific experimentation can tell us. The limitations of science predicated on assumptions about a stable reality is the type of "old thinking" that Joshua Cooper Ramo and Nassim Nicholas Taleb are critiquing. At the same time, Otto's defense of objective science is compelling. A key issue is understanding the nature of inquiry into the meanings ascribed to human and social experience. As Otto points out, some meanings are informed by long-established bodies of knowledge; others upon uninformed opinions. Being able to distinguish between the two forms of knowledge claims is paramount in any form of research.

Otto seems to imply, with either the objective knowledge of science or unsubstantiated beliefs and opinions? If these are our only choices, where does that leave interpretive, Scholar-Practitioner Inquiry? This is the conundrum Scholar-Practitioners need to think through as they craft a logic-of-justification for their studies. The starting point is to understand that interpretive studies yield a different form of knowledge that:

- Is context-dependent, not context independent;

- Draws upon concrete examples to illuminate abstract concepts;

- Is concerned with human interests and experience, traditions, institutions, etc.;

- Looks for nuanced interpretations of experience, not universal, causal, or predictive explanations;

- Seeks divergent rather than convergent points of view; and

- Is tentative and limited, not systematic, complete, or predictive.

If interpretive inquiry does not yield ideal theory or universally applicable laws, what should we call the knowledge generated through Scholar-Practitioner Inquiries? There is no universally agreed upon answer to this question. As indicated in Chapter 1, we prefer Barry Schwartz and Kenneth Sharpe's concept of practical wisdom. The deep learning associated with Scholar-Practitioner Inquiries yields insights that help Scholar Practitioners figure out "the right way to do the right thing in a particular circumstance, with a particular person, at a particular time." When the results of thoughtful Scholar-Practitioner Inquiries are shared, a growing storehouse of collective wisdom accumulates; wisdom that is useful in navigating the issues, problems, dilemmas, and predicaments[4] of complex practice.

---

4   To avoid awkward repetition of these forms of trouble, we will use "issue" as an umbrella descriptor.

Forms of Shared Wisdom

Wisdom does not accumulate simply by sharing the details of troubling situations. Wisdom comes from probing the situational details to:

- Identify the issue;
- Reveal the complexities embedded in the issue;
- Illuminate and critique the range of perspectives that have been brought to bear on the issue;
- Conceptualize the meaning(s) associated with the issue;
- Conceptualize a form for conveying those meanings to others.

The meanings generated through this process are more appropriately thought of as interpretive heuristics than ideal theory as characterized by Flyvbjerg and Otto. *The Fontana Dictionary of Modern Thought* defines heuristics in this way:

> In social science, the term is used especially to characterize conceptual devices such as ideal types, models, and working hypotheses which are not intended to describe or explain the facts, but to suggest possible explanations or eliminate others.[5]

In brief, heuristics are conceptual representations of complex phenomena, making them more understandable and amenable to further study. As indicated by *The Fontana Dictionary*, heuristics are used in science. For example, the formula "f = ma (force = mass x acceleration)" is a heuristic in the form of an equation grounded in a fundamental, scientifically-verified law of Newtonian physics.

In contrast, heuristics within the realm of Scholar-Practitioner Inquiry are grounded in the interpretative tradition of the arts and humanities. Common forms of *interpretive heuristics* include, but are

---

5   A. Bullock, O. Stallybrass, and S. Trmobley, eds. *The Fontana Dictionary of Modern Thought*, 2nd ed. (London: Fontana, 1988), 382.

not limited to, narratives/stories, fables, metaphors/similes, analogies, typologies, matrices, diagrams, figures, and policies. Consider Aesop's fable of the tortoise and the hare. It contains a moral lesson, not a law of behavior. Or consider what is communicated by the following two similes:

- Teaching is like a white-water rafting trip with no end to the rapids.
- Teaching is like gardening.[6]

Each conveys a different felt experience of teaching that can be probed for further meaning and implications; each conveys a mindset that is likely to influence a practitioner's attitude, actions, and decisions. Neither can be claimed as a fundamental law that can dictate rules of educational practice. Each can, however, convey certain wisdom about the nature of teaching.

Revisiting the Distinction Between Scientific Educational Research and Scholar-Practitioner Inquiry

In Chapter 1, we acknowledged our somewhat arbitrary distinction between research grounded in the world view of science and the world view of arts and humanities. At this point, in light of Shawn Otto's characterization of science as a collective endeavor, we call attention to a definition of educational research put forward by the American Educational Research Association (AERA):

> Education research is the scientific field of study that examines education and learning processes and the human attributes, interactions, organizations, and institutions that shape educational outcomes.[7]

---

6 Do you resonate with either (or both) of these similes? If so, that is an example of how wisdom about a shared human experience is conveyed. If not, what simile or metaphor for teaching would you use—if you are a teacher; if you are a principal or superintendent?

7 Retrieved from aera.net on May 7, 2020.

At first glance, this definition gave us pause, because it appears to negate almost 50 years of discourse on the legitimacy of alternatives to scientific educational research. During the 1970s and 1980s, heated debates occurred in AERA's journal and at its annual conference about questions such as: What could count as a dissertation; whether "science" encompassed all forms of inquiry; if research did not meet scientific criteria but reflected substantive scholarship, what should it be called? This struggle for language was not mere semantics. It was a struggle for recognition of a world view fundamentally different from science; what British scientist and novelist C.P. Snow characterized as two cultures— the culture of science and the culture of art.[8] Insistence on "science" as the overarching concept felt to many of us like a devaluing, not just of our work, but of our very way of being in the world. Having lived through those debates, we tend to be extra sensitive to the language of science; hence our initial misgivings about the AERA's definition.

Upon reflection, however, we think this definition may point, not to the nature of individual studies, but to the overall accumulation of knowledge as Otto describes it. Educational scholars—whether working in macro-contexts of educational systems or the micro-level of classrooms—all contribute to a shared knowledge of education as a field of study and a field of practice. As the results of studies are shared, their merits are critiqued by peers. What is deemed worthwhile is retained; what is deemed faulty disappears—perhaps not immediately, but eventually. For example, many different approaches to school reform have been tried. When research showed that an approach yielded no significant benefits, educational reformers tried a new approach which, in turn, was studied. Over the past two decades a great deal of money and effort was dedicated to the formation of privately managed charter schools. As Diane Ravitch points out in *Slaying Goliath*, mounting evidence has revealed deeply rooted flaws in this initiative. In the coming years, this ill-conceived reform effort will likely be replaced. Even now, the Carnegie Foundation is working with a process called "new improvement science" to achieve more effective schooling for all children. This is one example of how education as a scientific field

---

8 Stefan Collini, "Introduction," *The Two Cultures* by C.P. Snow (Cambridge, United Kingdom: Cambridge University Press, 1998), vii-viii.

advances by discarding unsubstantiated knowledge claims and entering into new cycles of inquiry.

Our intent is not to dismiss the importance and value of scientific educational research or to privilege Scholar-Practitioner Inquiry as a superior form of inquiry. Rather, our commitment is to help educational practitioners understand what form of research may best suit their world view and the practicalities of their circumstances. Further, we want Scholar-Practitioner Inquiries to be conducted with a level of rigor that contributes to the accumulating knowledge about quality education.

Judging Scholar-Practitioner Inquiry

In describing the painstaking process of accumulating scientific knowledge, Shawn Otto alludes to the peer review process. When scientists look at each other's work, they evaluate its merits based upon criteria embedded in the notion of "ideal theory." If these criteria cannot be applied to interpretive heuristics, we are not left with an anything-goes, free-for-all chaos of unsubstantiated beliefs and opinions. The logic-of-justification makes transparent the process through which the outcomes of the study are reached. The merits of the outcomes can then be judged on a set of criteria appropriate to interpretive Scholar-Practitioner Inquiry. Although there are no universally agreed upon criteria, we offer the following.

Useful. Scholar-Practitioners embark on an inquiry to gain a deeper understanding of a troubling experience; to gain insights that can guide decision making; to develop more nuanced responses to challenging situations. As a minimum, the results should be useful to the person conducting the inquiry. Beyond that, however, the results should contribute to established bodies of discourse relevant to clearly identifiable professional and/or scholarly audiences. If others look at the results, shrug their shoulders, and say "so what," the usefulness of the inquiry is called into question. By providing a logic about the intended audience for the study results, Scholar-Practitioners can forestall this criticism.

Educative. The usefulness of a study is tied to its power to educate—not in the sense of didactic prescriptions, but in offering new ways to think about troubling aspects of practice. If others read the results and say, "Wow, that's helpful. I never thought of it that way before," the study has been both educative and useful.

Well Warranted. Scholar-Practitioners provide thick, rich evidence to support their interpretations. Others might interpret the situation differently, but when the logics are clearly delineated, readers should be able to say, "I can see the thought process that led to this interpretation. I can see how they went from a specific starting point and arrived at this outcome." The author's thinking process is transparent, what Brent Kilbourn calls "self-conscious method."[1] This furthers the accumulation of knowledge as interpretations are critiqued and some found more useful and educative than others.

Verisimilitude. The writers' mantra of "show, don't tell" contributes to the quality Jerome Bruner characterizes as verisimilitude. The experiences that inform the study are richly descriptive, evoking a vicarious sense of participation in the events. Well-crafted experiential texts elicit responses such as, "How would I have reacted in such a situation?" or "That reminds me of the time when…" Accounts of experience succeed to the extent that others see the portrayed events as conceivable and believable.

Integrity. Scholar-Practitioners explicitly identify the genre within which they are working. The genre is congruent with interpretive inquiry. The inquirer follows the conventions of the genre or provides a rationale for departing from them. (We return to the concept of genre in the next chapter.)

Coherence. The heuristic portrayal has a cogent conceptual structure. The relationships among ideas represented by the heuristic are logical and clear. The written account of the study "hangs together"; it has a unity stemming from links among its underlying ideas and the development of thematic content.

Conceptually Compelling. This criterion speaks to the quality of thought that goes into the inquiry. The interpretations are carefully crafted from sufficiently thick and rich information. Reflection is done in a careful and systematic rather than haphazard fashion. Solipsistic,

---

1   Brent Kilbourn, "Fictional Theses in Educational Research," *Educational Researcher* 28, no 12 (1999): 28.

self-serving reasoning is avoided. There is sufficient depth of intellect to avoid superficial or simplistic reasoning. The study is important, meaningful, non-trivial; the results are insightful.

Ethical. Troubling experiences of practice often arise from interactions or relationships with others. As Scholar-Practitioners describe these experiences, others become "characters" in the stories being recounted—often without their knowledge or permission. This raises several ethical issues. Is it acceptable and fair to appropriate and represent others in service of one's own inquiry? Although it goes beyond the scope of this book to examine this complex issue, here are several points to consider:

- Has the inquirer avoided making claims about other individuals—their thoughts, feelings, personality, or character? In other words, does the inquirer understand that they are studying an issue, not specific individuals or groups of individuals? Are the knowledge claims about the issue, not an individual or group?

- Has the inquirer scrupulously avoided using their institutional power to force others to participate in their study?

- Unless permission has been granted by individuals, have the identities of others been appropriately and adequately protected?

- Has the inquirer avoided mean-spirited characterizations of others and avoided a "vendetta mentality"?

- Are ideas drawn from other sources cited?

Aesthetic. This quality is less relevant in fairly utilitarian studies (e.g., a policy statement). Studies that yield wisdom, however, often have an aesthetic quality, because they touch both mind and spirit. Thoughtful studies of particular experiences call forth universal dilemmas. Aesthetic representations have the power to move us; to unsettle the status quo; to change how we see ourselves, others, and the world. Thoughtful inquiries can lift us out of the mundane aggravations of daily practice and inspire us to imagine new possibilities. Let us be clear. Contrived attempts to be artistic fall short of this criterion. Mere decorative—artsy—touches for their own sake detract from the credibility of a study. Aesthetics emanate from the power, elegance, and insightfulness of one's thinking.

Revisiting the Relationship between Science and Art

In our efforts to tease out the nature of Scholar-Practitioner Inquiry, we have contrasted science to art. At a practical level of technique and procedure, this distinction can be helpful. When mindset is considered, the lines between science and art become porous, a point made quite eloquently by Shawn Otto:

> Science and art are intrinsically related and, in fact, were once one and the same. Both involve the detailed observation and representation of nature in its many aspects; both seek to capture and express some fundamental and perhaps ineffable truth. Both are concerned with the great questions of reality, of life, of an underlying order. Both require a sort of leisured study in a segregated place to maximize creativity, and both are driven forward by an intensely disciplined focus on the craft that can produce astounding bursts of creative insight. Physicists often talk about aesthetic qualities like beauty and symmetry, and indeed there is a long history of art apprehending the forms of nature later uncovered more explicitly by science. Great art and great science both produce a sense of wonderment, and the great artists and scientists are separated from the mediocre ones by the breadth of their minds and the originality of their ideas.[2]

Otto is talking about science and art at a grand scale. If we reframe his point in the realm of education, meritorious Scholar-Practitioner Inquiry is well within the capability of thoughtful professionals. We have been privileged to work with many practitioners whose deep learning resulted in studies that met the criteria outlined above. In addition to informing their own practice, these Scholar-Practitioners contributed to the wisdom so necessary for quality education.

---

2   Otto, 78.

SUMMARY

Our intent in this chapter has been to push beyond a focus on method as technique to the importance of understanding the epistemological, axiological, and ontological assumptions guiding one's method. Simplistically thinking of method only as technique (e.g., interviewing, questionnaires) runs the risk of meeting neither the criteria of scientific research nor Scholar-Practitioner Inquiry. Such "non-studies" reflect poorly on the student, and possibly on the whole idea of Scholar-Practitioner Inquiry as illustrated by *Scenario 2.1*.

In outlining the above criteria, we used the concept of "genre" in relation to the integrity of a study. When Scholar-Practitioners follow the conventions of a particular inquiry genre, their logic-of-justification is clearer and stronger. We acknowledge that the concept of "genre" is not commonly used when talking about method. For that reason, we explore that concept in the next chapter.

As you progress in your studies, seek out opportunities to serve as a reviewer of journal articles or conference presentation proposals. This will give you deeper insight into the criteria used to judge scholarly work.

SCENARIO 2.1
CAUGHT BETWEEN WORLD VIEWS

Is there a legitimate alternative to scientific research?

COMMENTARY

This anecdote was shared by a doctoral student during an introductory course on qualitative research.

I was really excited when I registered for this class. I was really looking forward to it, then I made an egregious error—I told a work colleague what I was studying this semester and got lambasted. POW! You see, the doctor I work with is one of this country's most respected researchers in my field. He has published hundreds of peer-reviewed research articles in some of the most prestigious journals in medicine. He was the editor of a peer-reviewed journal that was "ruined" by qualitative research. He snarled, ""There is no such thing as qualitative research. It is an oxymoron. I cannot believe that a journal would publish an article citing interviews with earthquake survivors who all say 'it was terrible' and call that research!" I really like and respect this doctor, so his critique really took the wind out of my sails.

COMMENTARY (CONTINUED)

This brief anecdote illustrates several important points. First, although the student is interested in exploring "qualitative" inquiry, his colleague believes there is no such thing. With his scientific mindset, the physician defines legitimate research by conventions that the authors of the paper apparently violated—hence the judgment "qualitative research" is an oxymoron.

Second, before we dismiss the physician's harsh criticism, it is important to consider whether the authors of the journal article violated the conventions of good qualitative research. The study may have, in fact, been an oxymoron if the researchers invested time, effort, and money to find out only that earthquake survivors described the experience as terrible. Scholars in both a scientific and an interpretive tradition would find such a study to be unworthy of publication. (Consider a more recent example from the COVID-19 pandemic. If researchers did a study and learned only that people found the experience stressful, we might be inclined to share the physician's opinion.) A key safeguard against this type of flawed study is understanding the world view from which a study is conducted.

Third, the physician represents a community of physician-researchers that the student respects. Presumably he wants to complete an inquiry that will be respected by that community. If he decides to pursue a qualitative inquiry, then he needs to offer a clear and cogent rationale for doing so. If he does so, perhaps he can help his physician colleague to see the merits of qualitative research. Or, perhaps not. For this reason, it is important for the student to seek out research communities within his field, communities that understand the nature of good qualitative (interpretive) research.

Fourth, the anecdote raises the question of what criteria the journal editors used to deem the article worthy of publication. This was a peer reviewed journal. Did the reviewers better understand the conventions of qualitative research than the physician? Did the editors run a calculated risk of publishing an article that would challenge assumptions about scientific research? Or did the journal editors make a mistake in accepting a poorly conducted study for publication?

Of course, we can't know the answers to these questions, but we can speculate. This anecdote took place when qualitative research was just emerging in fields of education and health care. The conventions were not yet clearly defined, so judging the quality of the work was often difficult. Sometimes journal editors would accept an article because they wanted to support alternative modes of research even though they might not be sure about the merits of the piece. Since then a great deal of progress has been made by scholars who follow the conventions of interpretive inquiry. Indeed, using the term "interpretive" rather than "qualitative" has become a convention for many who draw upon the arts and humanities for their research genre.

Several additional points are worth flagging. The student's anecdote represents an experiential text—a micro-narrative if you will. Our commentary illustrates how such texts can serve as a springboard for raising issues. We have tried to be mindful of what claims we can make. We cannot, for example, claim to know what the physician, student, or journal editors <u>really</u> understand about qualitative research. We can speculate about possible positions they represent, not to make judgments about them, but to illustrate highly complex and abstract aspects of Scholar-Practitioner Inquiry.

In a sense, when others share a text of their experience, we are appropriating their stories to serve our inquiry purposes. Respecting these stories, using them in good faith to explore important issues, generating useful, educative, and compelling insights—these are ethical issues in Scholar-Practitioner Inquiry. We knew a teacher, for example, who collected stories from her students and then made claims about the students to support her own pre-conceptions and biases. This is a misappropriation of stories, because the teacher's interpretation of the stories offered little insight into the pedagogical issue she claimed to be studying.

SCENARIO 2.2
CAUGHT BETWEEN WORLD VIEWS

How do we get to the heart of the matter?

COMMENTARY

The following anecdote was described by Marcy, a doctoral student who was working as an assistant in the research and evaluation department of a large urban school district.

My assignment was to develop a survey of opinions our staff held about the personnel department. It seems that there had been some dissonance between the personnel department and the rest of the staff. The board of directors asked for clarification of the issues. Well, I didn't really know what the nature of the disagreements was. I didn't know much about what the personnel department did either, so I began to talk with people. I did formal interviews; I had conversations over lunch with people from both groups; I talked to people in the elevators. I listened to their stories about important incidents. By the time I constructed the items for the survey, I knew more about the personnel department and the situation with staff than I ever imagined. It was rich stuff. Somehow, when I began to put it into abstract form for the items of the survey, it was lifeless and didn't really get to the heart of the matter.

My boss really only believes that quantitative data is full-blown, or maybe, hard, research. If I report the results of the narrative data, that would only be my interpretations. The survey would verify that the respondents really hold certain views. It would be more objective. I'm really frustrated, though, because the findings on the survey don't get to the heart of the matter. They just don't get to the heart of the issues.

COMMENTARY (CONTINUED)

Marcy and her boss value different forms of knowledge about the problems in the personnel department. Given her boss's position and responsibilities, his primary concern may be to determine the scope of the problem(s). In this case, he does need the numbers in order to verify that a sufficient number of people are unhappy with the personnel department to warrant corrective measures. If the complaints are coming from a few disgruntled employees, a far different administrative response is called for than if the complaints are widespread.

Marcy, as a good evaluator, values knowledge that goes beyond what the numbers will tell her. Even if a survey verified that 100% of the employees are unhappy with the personnel department, little insight would be gained unless the survey questions began to tease out the underlying issues. To develop a reliable and valid questionnaire, Marcy began to seek information about various complaints from multiple sources. By the time she had enough information to construct the survey questions, she also doubted that the survey would be as useful as her boss imagines.

Let's say that Marcy developed ten questions, each of which captured an employee concern. Then she constructed a 5-point rating scale to determine how serious employees consider each problem to be. Suppose the results indicated (depending on the specific question) 25 – 50% of the respondents consider the problems to be "somewhat or very serious." As Marcy pointed out, knowing the numbers would not provide sufficient insight to know what corrective actions might be appropriate. For this, more nuanced information would be necessary, the very type of information Marcy had been gathering through her formal and informal conversations with employees.

Marcy seems to feel at an impasse with her boss. She doesn't see much point in going through the motions of a survey that won't yield substantive insights that allow for action. He doesn't trust what he probably considers to be unreliable anecdotal information. This is not an uncommon dilemma facing Scholar-Practitioners—individually and collectively. At the heart of the impasse lies a difference in world views.

CHAPTER 3

Inquiry Genre as Logic-of-Justification

CLAIMING A GENRE

In Chapter 2, we suggested criteria for evaluating the quality of Scholar-Practitioner Inquiries. We also alluded to the concept of "genre" as a framework within which to lay out the logics of one's study. Analogies from the world of sports can illustrate the meaning of genre.

Those who play football need to know more than the techniques of passing or blocking. Understanding football comprises a complex constellation of rules that govern what counts as legitimate and successful play. A very different constellation of rules governs what counts as legitimate play in other sports such as baseball, soccer, hockey, tennis, golf, or gymnastics. The descriptor "interpretive inquiry" is analogous to the descriptor "ballgames." Particular types of interpretive inquiry—what we call genre—are analogous to specific sports. Each has its own conventions and internal logic.

Integrity is one of the criteria we suggested for Scholar-Practitioner Inquiry. This quality is achieved by following the conventions of the genre one has claimed for a study. Just as football coaches can draw upon many conventions to formulate a game plan, they would not last long in the National Football League if they suddenly had their punter use a bat. It simply would not be logical. Following the conventions of a particular genre creates a logical structure for whatever inquiry "game" one is claiming to play.

Just as no two football games are identical, no two Scholar-Practitioner Inquiries are identical. Yet in both instances a recognized set of conventions is used to carry out a "game plan" and achieve a desired goal. On Monday mornings across the United States football enthusiasts will spend hours debating the logic of going for a touchdown rather than a field goal on 4th down. Or they may intricately dissect the call to pass rather than run the ball on a particular play. They might say more or less politely, "What the heck was the coach thinking?" Such Monday morning quarterbacking has been enhanced by video clips of the plays under scrutiny. Those videos provide a stable record of the action. Coaches, like their fans, can review and critique the rationale for their game plan and judge how well it worked out.

Dissertations, theses, and capstone projects borne of Scholar-Practitioner Inquiries are stable records of the inquirers' "game plan." They explain not only what was done, but why. They provide the logic behind each move of the inquiry. Just as fans and coaches can critique the logic behind a football game, scholars and practitioners in one's field can critique the logic behind a Scholar-Practitioner Inquiry.

Among the more common genre suited to Scholar-Practitioner Inquiry are narrative, case study, action research, investigative journalism, and grounded theory. At this point, you might be wondering, "How do I choose a genre?" In response, we return to our sports analogy. How did Dan Marino "choose" football? How did Michael Jordan "choose" basketball; or Lyndsey Vonn skiing; Serena Williams tennis; Mario Lemieux hockey; Mia Hamm soccer; Simone Biles gymnastics; Tiger Woods golf? We venture to say no one gave them a list of options and said, "Choose one." Rather, as they engaged in their respective sports, their latent talents emerged, and they claimed the sport for which they were uniquely suited. It is here that our sports analogy seems to break down. After all, each of these athletes had opportunities from early childhood to engage in sports and realize their talent. Most Scholar-Practitioners have not been preparing from childhood to engage in a formal inquiry. Or have they?

All of us have innate ways of making meaning of experience. Some of us may think in images, like our colleague, Doug Conlan, who doodles while he is thinking. The doodles are not simply random scribbles. Rather, they are pictures that capture what he is thinking or feeling. Our colleague Wendy Milne keeps an artist's sketch pad handy and creates pencil and ink drawings when she is trying to sort through a troubling thought or situation.

As developmental psychologist James Fowler notes, images may precede our ability to express concerns in conceptual terms.

> An image, as I use the term here, begins as a vague, felt inner representation of some state of affairs and of our feelings about it. As we have suggested, the forming of an image does not wait or depend upon conscious processes. The image unites "information" and feeling, it holds together orientation and affectional significance. As such, images are prior to and deeper than concepts. When we are asked what we think or know about something or someone, we call up our images, setting in motion a kind of scanning interrogation or questioning of them. Then in a process that involves both a forming and an expression, we narrate what our images "know." The narration may take story form; it may take poetic or symbolic form, transforming nascent inner images into articulated, shared images; or it may take the propositional form of conceptual abstractions.[1]

Think about the ways in which you sort through confusing situations or troubling experiences. How do images come to you? Perhaps they emerge as you take a walk, work out at the gym, or meditate. Perhaps you keep a journal or write poetry. Or listen to music. Or talk with a close friend. Or audio record your musings. Some individuals think in narrative, or metaphors, or analogies.

If we have been lucky, we have been encouraged to develop these ways of making meaning. If not, we may have to reclaim neglected talents from our childhood. As you peruse books or articles on various genre, many may seem suited to the question you plan to study. "Choosing" among these options may be a matter of claiming one for which you are well suited.

---

1   James W. Fowler. *Stages of Faith: The Psychology of Human Development and the Quest for Meaning* (San Francisco: Harper & Row, 1981). 26.

Situating a Logic-of-Justification within a Genre

As you explore, be aware that there are multiple schools of thought about any given genre. For example, a case study may be embedded in the scientific tradition of medicine or the disciplines of sociology and anthropology (See *Scenario 3.1*). Narrative has roots both in social sciences and literature (*Scenario 3.2*). Action research has a long history, and its conventions have evolved over time. Some authors view grounded theory from a scientific perspective; others from an interpretive perspective (See *Scenario 3.3*). In short, not all sources of information about various genre will be consistent. Part of your logic-of-justification will be sorting through which sources are most suited to you and the study you want to conduct. For this, we return briefly to our sports analogy.

It is our contention that each genre, like various forms of ballgames, embodies its own set of conventions. These conventions have evolved over time within particular philosophical and disciplinary traditions. Language specific to each genre has evolved to express the conventions. Football, for example, uses a language of *downs, goalposts, holding, kickoffs*, and *referees*; baseball uses a language of *strikes, home runs, bases, outs*, and *umpires*. A language for explaining interpretive inquiry continues to emerge, but has yet to reach general agreement. Different authors use different descriptors, which can complicate the task of acquiring a language for Scholar-Practitioner Inquiry. We use the following language to convey the logics associated with interpretive inquiry versus scientific research.

- Interpretive inquiry rather than scientific research[2]
- Intent of the inquiry to be fulfilled rather than hypothesis to be tested
- Guiding questions as distinct from data gathering questions
- Genre (logic-of-justification) rather than method (as procedure and technique)
- Text rather than data

---

2 We make this distinction cautiously because at its finest the line between science and art begins to blur.

- Interpretation rather than analysis
- Results or insights rather than findings
- Portrayal rather than data display

Although you may make meaning through non-linguistic modalities, eventually you will need language to express the logics of your study. In this regard, language entails more than just the words you choose, but also the stance, position, and voice from which you write. These, too, must be consistent with the conventions of your genre. For this it is useful to shift our analogy from sports to literature.

Conventions of Writing in Interpretive Genre

Conventions of Structure. Although different literary genre may not be as immediately apparent as different sports, most individuals are able to distinguish a play from a poem, a short story from a novel, a documentary from a science fiction film. Each type of literary work has certain structural characteristics that distinguish it as a particular genre. Creating a movie script entails conventions that are quite different from creating a collection of poems or essays.

For decades, the format of a thesis and dissertation followed the conventional structure of a science report:

- Chapter 1—Introduction
- Chapter 2—Review of literature that demonstrated the significance of the research being proposed—i.e., how would it extend current theoretical knowledge; hypothesis to be tested
- Chapter 3—Description of the research methods as procedures
- Chapter 4—Presentation of data analysis
- Chapter 5—Discussion and conclusions[3]

Over the past 50 years, as Scholar-Practitioners pushed the boundaries of what constitutes a thesis or dissertation, the standard

---

3 Scientific journal articles also followed this format, albeit in a more condensed form.

structure of the science report was often too confining. Some began to structure dissertations as scholarly books. Some argued that a dissertation could take the form of a novel. With a growing emphasis on scholarly practice, attention became focused on formats to make the dissertation results more accessible to practitioners. For example, a dissertation consisting of publishable articles might be structured with an introductory chapter, a separate chapter for each article, and a final chapter reflecting on what the author learned as a result of the inquiry. Similarly, a policy-oriented dissertation might have an introductory chapter followed by a chapter for each policy, and a final reflective chapter.

Structuring a dissertation to convey the meanings of an interpretive inquiry is a creative act. Like an artist whose work renders a particular view of a subject, Scholar-Practitioners are rendering their particular view of the issue under study. This act of conceptual creation lies at the very heart of interpretive inquiry and is the most challenging part of the entire inquiry process.[4]

Conventions of Stance, Positionality, and Voice. Briefly stated, these three conventions underpin the aspects of writing style:

- Stance—the relationship that one has toward what and/or who is being studied;
- Positionality—the lenses through which you interpret that which is under study, and
- Voice—the tone with which you write.

Because those working within the world view of science claim a stance of objectivity and a position of neutrality, they write in an impersonal, third person voice. Because interpretive inquiries offer meanings constructed by a particular individual from a particular position, it is more appropriate to write in the first person. Think back to the example of the Chinese student whose advisor deemed the study unacceptable because the student could not claim a stance of objectivity

---

4 For a resource for understanding issues of portrayal, see *The Authority to Imagine: The Struggle toward Representation in Dissertation Writing*, edited by Noreen B. Garman and Maria Piantanida (Pittsburgh: Learning Moments Press, 2018.)

or a position of neutrality. If she proceeded with the study against her advisor's advice and then wrote in the third person, it would create a fundamental mismatch between the nature of her study and how she portrays it. On the other hand, if she claimed a stance of interpretive inquiry, acknowledged her position as a Chinese student, and wrote in the first person, the logics of her study would be aligned.

Scholar-Practitioners engaged in interpretive inquiries strengthen the coherence of their writing when they are aware of the position from which they are working and make conscious decisions about stance and voice.

To return briefly to our sports analogy, imagine the reaction of Monday morning quarterbacks if someone started talking about home runs instead of touchdowns or "knocking the ball out of the field" instead of "putting it through the goal posts." Their language would clearly reveal they did not know what they were talking about. Without understanding the writing conventions of interpretive inquiry, Scholar-Practitioners run the risk of revealing a fundamental lack of understanding about what "game" they are playing.

In terms of stance, interpretive inquirers shy away from the term "subject" to describe others who are involved in their studies. Subject implies an entity being scrutinized by an outsider, often one with greater power over the entity under study. In interpretive inquiries, the terms "participant," "co-participant," or "informant" tend to be used when describing individuals who share their personal experience or expertise with the investigator. Inter-subjectivity tends to be used when meanings of multiple participants are involved in a study. Collaborative or cooperative tend to describe studies embedded in settings where information is being gathered from multiple sources. We tend to use the term "contextualized" to characterize Scholar-Practitioner Inquiries of practice.

Keep in mind that these descriptions are conventions, not rules. Scholar-Practitioners will need to give some thought to terminology that most accurately describes their relationship to the setting of their study and any individuals involved.

Another aspect of stance indicates the relationship Scholar-Practitioners claim toward the knowledge they are putting forward. Our wedding of "scholar" with "practitioner" connotes a particular stance of deep learning within and about one's context of practice. Other stances that have been claimed by Scholar-Practitioners include "eyewitness," "public intellectual," "citizen scientist," "steward of the profession," and "educational advocate." Some Scholar-Practitioners might adopt the stance of skeptic if, for example, they want to study a policy of dubious merit. Others, particularly those working in arts-based genre of interpretive inquiry, have claimed the stance of connoisseur (one with a finely honed sensitivity to nuances). Stances that tend to undermine the credibility of Scholar-Practitioner Inquiries include zealous cheering for a particular practice or negative criticism (as opposed to thoughtful critique). Claiming a stance of "expert" can be risky. On one hand, thoughtful practiced-embedded studies can engender a greater expertise. On the other hand, it can connote a level of certitude at odds with interpretive inquiry.

Positionality refers to two constellations of information. One encompasses personal attributes that go beyond one's professional role. These include attributes like:

- Gender/Sexual orientation
- Race/ethnicity
- Socio-economic status
- Political ideology

Acknowledging these attributes may be more or less important depending on the nature of the study. Again, we flag these as aspects of logic of justification that may need deliberate attention.

The other constellation of information relates to one's professional role, experience, and expertise. Are you writing from the position of beginning or experienced practitioner, teacher or administrator, public school educator, or higher education faculty?

Voice—the tone in which one writes—often provides insight into the author's stance and position. For example, Scholar-Practitioners often strive for a reflective, contemplative, serious, earnest, or thoughtful tone rather than a didactic, authoritative, or judgmental tone. Tones that reflect curiosity and speculation are more consistent with a stance of interpretive inquiry than declarative or judgmental tones. Temperate, conciliatory, invitational tones ask readers to join in a process of exploration. Writing with a passionate tone is a delicate proposition. On one hand, it can reinforce the seriousness or urgency of an issue. Diane Ravitch's tone in *Slaying Goliath*, for example, is certainly passionate and could be seen as a polemic (i.e., an aggressive attack on or refutation of the opinions or principles of others). But she has the knowledge and facts to argue a passionate case against those who want to privatize public education. In less capable hands, polemics can just come across as strident rants with little educative value. That's the risk inexperienced Scholar-Practitioners take when trying too hard to express their frustrations.

SUMMARY

The ways in which voice, stance, and positionality are dealt with can contribute to or undermine the credibility of a study. When stance, positionality, and voice are congruent with the conventions of a genre, they contribute to the authenticity, integrity, and trustworthiness of a study. Inconsistencies among stance, positionality, and voice raise doubts about the author's understanding of the genre and inquiry tradition. *Scenario 3.4* illustrates several points about stance, position, and voice.

One way to check on these qualities is to read drafts of a study aloud, listening carefully to the tone that comes across. Even better is sharing drafts with others who can provide feedback on how the stance, positionality, and voice strike them. Cultivating a style of writing congruent with interpretive inquiry can take time and practice. Often writing classes focus on more functional forms of writing (think the five paragraph essay). Writing in interpretive inquiries is often the way in which meanings are constructed. During the Exploratory Phase and beyond, it is useful to read widely, paying attention to stance, positionality, and voice. Finding those with whom you resonate can help you develop a more acutely attuned ear for your own writing.

SCENARIO 3.1
HYPOTHETICAL EXAMPLE
OF CASE STUDIES

This is one of two scenarios in the book that are not based on our own experiences or those shared with us by others. We debated about the appropriateness of drawing upon the tragedy of school shootings for this hypothetical example. In the end, we decided to include it to illustrate a number of issues, the first of which is the ethical implications of context embedded studies. On more than one occasion, we have met students who thought that doing a case study of their own classroom, school, or district would give them convenient access to information. Convenience, however, needs to be weighed against the ethics of making public what others might want to keep private. Although Lynn Richards conducted a narrative, not case study, of her pedagogy, she obtained permission from the parents of every student in her classroom before beginning her inquiry. (See *Scenario 6.2.*) This was complex enough, but imagine the ethical complications of studying a school or district. Certainly, the school board would have to give consent and would probably consult the district's attorney. Even with that approval, individuals within the school or district might resent or even oppose being studied. Using pseudonyms for individuals and the district is a common convention in case studies, but really offers little anonymity when details make it clear who or what is being described. Without the details, the study might lack verisimilitude. With details, individual rights to privacy might be violated. This is anything but "convenient."

Another point illustrated by this example is the evolving nature of knowledge within a field of study.

Someone studying school violence 25 years ago would have found few, if any, references to mass shootings. Sadly, since then, a growing body of literature has evolved. Early on, the importance of a study might have been challenged because a scale of violence beyond bullying was unimaginable. Now the challenge would be to justify how a new study would contribute important enough insights to intrude upon (some might say exploit) a tragedy.

Third, the following hypothetical examples illustrate the point that conventions of a genre can vary from one discourse community to another. It is not enough to say, "I'm doing a case study (or narrative or grounded theory)." Case study offers a particularly rich set of variations among case study conventions within different disciplines. From the decision to draw upon conventions of case study in a particular field, to setting the boundaries of the case, to deciding what sources of information to tap, to deciding how to gather that information—each decision requires a rationale. By making the rationale transparent, the researcher allows others to see how and why the case study was crafted in a particular way and how this way contributes to the outcomes of the study.

Fourth, because Scholar-Practitioner Inquiries are context specific, defining the context is a key aspect of a study. Setting boundaries—framing the case—makes clear what is under study, a point we hope becomes clearer in the following hypothetical options.

Option 1. A Case Study of a School Shooter. This frames the case around one person. A researcher asking this question might follow the conventions of a medical case study, psychiatry in particular. Building the case might include information gathered from parents, neighbors, students, teachers, counselors, etc. The aim would be to better understand an individual shooter. The outcomes of the study might be useful to school counselors and psychologists, giving them a more nuanced framework for meeting the needs of troubled students.

Option 2. A Case Study of a Mass Shooting at a Particular School. This frames the shooting as an incident within a particular social setting. The conventions of case study in the fields of sociology or anthropology might guide the study. With this frame, the shooter is one of many "elements" in the case. Information for this case might include socio-economic data about the school's community; the size of the student body; accounts of the incident from students, teachers, administrators, support staff, and first responders. The intent of the study would be to render as complete and detailed description of the event as possible. Information from different sources would be compared to establish a timeline of the event—when and how it started, proceeded, and ended. The outcome of such a study might be helpful to administrators and law enforcement personnel as they consider ways to create safer school environments.

Option 3. A Case Study of a Teacher's Pedagogical Response to a School Shooting. This frames the case around one person, who is studying her own experience before and after the shooting. She could set the case in the class period she was teaching when the shooting occurred. Or she could set it in the broader context of all her classes. For this study, the teacher might draw from the conventions of educational case studies as described by Robert Stake. Information to construct the case might come from her own journal, a comparison of lesson plans before and after the shooting, articles about other school shootings, literature on the effects of violence and trauma. On one hand, the intent of such a case study might be to generate pedagogical insights that could be helpful to other educators. At a deeper level it might be the teacher's way of coping with a traumatic experience, and therefore might be helpful to others who have been traumatized by violence.

Option 4. A Case Study of School Shootings. In this case, a social phenomenon is at the center of the study. The conventions of investigative journalism might guide such a study. A quick Google search of "school shootings" provides a depressingly long list of shootings that happen in and around schools. This would prompt the researcher to clarify the type of shooting that defines the case. The intent of such a study might be to document the escalation of school violence as an indicator of a broader social problem and call attention to the need for legislative action to ameliorate the underlying problems.

Option 5. A Case Study of Student Responses to a Mass Shooting in a School. This shifts the frame of the case to students. Depending on the intent of the study, the focus could be on students who became anti-gun activists, or it could look at the differences between the activist students and those who chose not to engage in activism. Setting the parameters of the case would entail a decision to study student responses in one district or multiple districts where shootings had occurred. The logic-of-justification would include a rationale for how many districts and what districts were chosen for the study. A similar case study might put parental responses at the center of the case. Such a study might blend conventions from sociological case studies and investigative journalism. The aim of such a case study might be to provide the general public with a deeper understanding of a social problem.

Option 6. A Case Study for (or against) Arming Teachers to Increase School Safety. With this framing, a policy issue lies at the heart of the case. The conventions of legal cases might be used to lay out the arguments for and against this particular safety strategy. Information for building the case might come from mental health and law enforcement experts, districts that did or did not choose to arm teachers, and other research that examined factors contributing to a school shooting. The audience for such a study might be school board members, school administrators, local governing bodies, or the general public.

SCENARIO 3.2
HYPOTHETICAL EXAMPLES
OF NARRATIVE INQUIRY

Just as case studies can be framed in many different ways, so, too, can narrative inquiries. Robert Nash's view of personal narrative is embedded in a literary tradition. Scholar Laurel Richardson's[5] view leans towards a social science perspective; she offers us a useful typology ranging from the personal to the cultural.

Certainly, the COVID-19 pandemic constitutes a troubling moment, not just for individual educators, but for our country as a whole. Embedded in this historic moment are a multitude of issues that bear careful study. Therefore, to illustrate different forms of narrative, we draw upon the troubling moment precipitated by the COVID-19 pandemic.

Narratives of Everyday Life articulate "...how actors go about their rounds and accomplish their tasks." Scholar-Practitioners' stories in this vein might describe how a teacher, administrator, speech, or occupational therapist altered their daily practice. What schedule did they establish? What new channels of communication were used? What tasks were put on hold? What new tasks needed attention? Imagine responding to the question, "What did you do in school today?" Perhaps for a while every day was different as adjustments were made until a new routine could be established. Sharing these stories of everyday life can provide useful ideas to others.

Autobiographical Narratives articulate "...how the past is related to the present. Events have a beginning, a middle, and an end." Such a narrative might have a title like, "How I Survived the COVID Pandemic of 2020." In this form of narrative, Scholar-Practitioners could draw upon a series of Everyday Life stories and weave them into a broader, more cohesive story. Such Autobiographic Narratives would move beyond an accounting of daily actions and provide insight into what the authors learned about themselves, how they think about their practice, and how they cope with unexpected disruptions.

---

5 Laurel Richardson, *Writing Strategies: Reaching Diverse Audiences.* Qualitative Research Methods Series 21 (Newbury Park, CA: Sage, 1990).

Biographical Narratives articulate an author's "…understanding of other people's lives…Social interaction depends upon actors making sense of others' actions and motivations from *the point of view* of the others, from their biographical perspective." Teachers, for example, might gather stories from students and/or parents about their experience of "schooling at home." Principals might gather stories from teachers to understand the nature of support that was more or less helpful. Superintendents might gather stories from school board members to better understand their concerns. In shaping a study, decisions would need to be made about whose stories to gather. For example, teachers might want to gather stories from other teachers in their district, or those who teach the same subject or grade level in other districts. In this form of narrative inquiry, great attention is given to the accuracy with which the stories of others are portrayed. Often, the researcher will share a draft of the biography with the study participant so that any misrepresentations or inaccuracies can be corrected.

Cultural Narratives have sociological significance. "Cultural stories provide exemplars of lives, heroes, villains, and fools and they are embedded in larger cultural and social frameworks as well as stories about home, community, society, and humankind." Richardson maintains that cultural narratives are typically told from the perspective of those with "ruling interests," and so tend to maintain the status quo. Examples of cultural narratives include those such as "our schools are failing," "schools need to prepare children with workplace skills," "quality education makes us a competitive world power," "every child should have access to a quality education," "education can ameliorate poverty." Many scholars study these cultural stories to understand the forces that have shaped them and what effects they have. During the early and most severe days of the pandemic, our cultural narratives about the health care system were shaken. As one pundit put it, "We've drawn back the curtain and exposed the inadequacies of our system." Less media attention was given to the ways in which the pandemic disrupted education narratives. But as the school year ended, media stories began to emerge around the cultural rituals of graduation— teachers and administrators who hand delivered diplomas; celebrities who broadcast graduation messages; YouTube videos of graduation speeches, etc.

Collective Narratives give "voice to those who are silenced or marginalized in the cultural narrative." Educational scholars conduct studies that challenge the cultural narratives. Advocacy groups, for example, articulate narratives that challenge "the deficit model of special education" or the negative stereotypes of various minority groups. A colleague of ours studied stereotypes about women as school administrators by collecting "incredible tales." The idea for her dissertation emerged as various colleagues would say to her, "You won't believe this, but..." What followed would be an outrageous assumption about why women couldn't possibly be good administrators. As she commented at the end of the study, "The problem wasn't getting enough of these stories for the dissertation. It was getting friends and colleagues to stop sending them to me." One problematic of collective narrative studies is the presumption that one can give voice to others. While this seems admirable, it is predicated on a sense of superiority or superior power, as though others can't speak for themselves. This has led some scholars to shift their language from "giving voice" to "making space for voices to be heard." A variety of narrative conventions have emerged to make clearer whose story is being told and by whom. The COVID-19 pandemic disrupted many cultural narratives about the way school is supposed to be conducted in our country. This creates a fertile ground in which alternative collective narratives can be put forward. One of the narratives we find particularly compelling is the role of Scholar-Practitioners in reform efforts. Perhaps there has never been a better time to challenge old narratives that teachers must be improved by top-down, externally imposed strategies.

The preceding notes illustrate just a few of the many variations on narrative as an inquiry genre. Those considering narrative as a genre will find a wealth of resources to inform their thinking—resources about narrative as a method and examples of narratives written by and about teachers and administrators.

On a final note, we venture to say that everyone has a story to tell about their time during the pandemic. Many of these stories have intertwining themes of coping with educational issues as a professional and as a parent of school-age children. Whether or not you intend to conduct a formal Scholar-Practitioner Inquiry, whether or not you would claim narrative as your genre, recording these stories while they are still fresh is important. Regardless of how well one adapted to the challenges presented by distance education, the stories provide an important foundation upon which more formal studies can build.

SCENARIO 3.3
SCIENTIFIC VERSUS INTERPRETIVE
GROUNDED THEORY

COMMENTARY

This Scenario comes from the work of Robin Grubs, who teaches genetic counseling in a school of public health where scientific research tends to be the default mode for dissertations. Because Robin knew her committee members might not be familiar with the details of grounded study, she felt a need to clarify the logics of her study, for herself as much as her committee. Robin reports that, as she read the literature, she began to see two contesting schools of thought about grounded theory—one situated in the post-positivist view of science, the other in the interpretive tradition.

Grounded theory emerged as a research method (genre) when qualitative research was beginning to filter into fields of practice. It especially appealed to those working in the health sciences, because it gave clear procedures for analyzing qualitative data and formulating a theory "grounded in" the data. At times, scientific researchers who are conducting survey research will use grounded theory as a data analysis technique to reduce and convert large masses of qualitative data into numeric patterns. From our perspective, this misses the power of grounded theory as a process for generating theoretical constructs.

The more Robin tried to determine which school of thought was "the right one," the more elusive that answer became. Eventually, she stopped looking for the right answer out in the literature and thought carefully about what she wanted to understand. This led her to claim an interpretive logic-of-justification for grounded theory. The chart on the following page helps to illustrate the relationship between underlying world view assumptions and aspects of the study.

The row titled "Method," alludes to three procedures within the grounded theory genre. *Coding* and *constant comparative analysis* refer to the process by which researchers identify key concepts in the qualitative data and map relationships among them. *Memoing* is the process by which researchers record their impressions, speculations, insights, and evolving interpretation about the codes.

TWO DIFFERENT APPROACHES TO A GROUNDED THEORY STUDY OF A GENETIC COUNSELING ISSUE		
Issue	**Post-Positive World View**	**Interpretive World View**
Purpose of the Study	To identify factors associated with women's/couples' decision to accept or reject prenatal testing.	To understand the meanings that women/couples ascribe to the offer of prenatal genetic counseling and testing.
Purpose of Research	To generate scientific knowledge of relationships between factor(s) and decision outcomes	To generate interpretive heuristics of meanings ascribed to experience
What is valued as legitimate knowledge (Axiological assumption)	Generalized patterns of factors that influence decisions about genetic counseling and prenatal testing	Insights into the existential experience of facing a pregnancy in which there is a risk of genetic abnormality.
Relationship between Research & Practice (Ontological assumption)	Factors would help practitioners to differentiate between clients who would and would not accept testing and allow them to develop strategies to assist both groups in the decision making process.	Insights into the existential experience allow the counselor to be more present to and empathetic with clients in the counseling encounter.
Reality (Ontological assumption)	Discrete factors or combinations of factors that influence a client's/patient's biomedical decision	Biomedical decisions have existential meanings that cannot be reduced to component variables.

Two Different Approaches to a Grounded Theory Study of a Genetic Counseling Issue		
Issue	**Post-Positive World View**	**Interpretive World View**
Knowledge of reality (Epistemological assumption)	Lies in verification of factors that generalize across a population faced with the decision of accepting or rejecting genetic counseling/testing	Lies in understanding & acknowledging the meanings individuals ascribe to experience of being at risk and accepting/rejecting genetic counseling/ testing; such knowledge is always partial & tentative
Knowledge claims (Epistemological assumption)	Factors that can be generalized to a population of patients	Heuristics that help practitioners respond empathetically and wisely to client concerns
Researcher Position	Genetic Counselor as Scientific Researcher	Genetic Counselor as Practitioner-Researcher
Researcher Values (Axiological assumption)	Commonalities among clients; common denominators	Diversity/idiosyncrasy of individual clients
Language/voice of researcher	Propositional, formal, professional/technical	Narrative, conversational, accessible
Stance of researcher	Objective, detached	Intersubjective, engaged
Conditions of the Study	Decontextualized; reductionistic; identification and control of discrete variables associated with a particular decision; consistency of data collection and analysis procedures	Contextualized within storied accounts of client experience; holistic; flexibility in collection of experiential texts; researcher interpretation of texts

TWO DIFFERENT APPROACHES TO A GROUNDED THEORY STUDY OF A GENETIC COUNSELING ISSUE		
Issue	**Post-Positive World View**	**Interpretive World View**
Individuals participating in study	Subjects	Informants
Materials used to generate research results	Data sets often generated through structured or semi-structured interviews. Emphasis on standardizing a protocol for asking questions and recording answers. In recent years, video recording of interviews has become more common in an effort to create a valid and verifiable record of the data gathering process.	Texts generated through conversational interviews. The interviewer has overall objectives for the interview, but follows the lead of the informant. It is assumed that questions will vary based on issues that arise in the conversation. Trust is placed in the theoretical sensitivity of the researcher to hear and pursue generative ideas emerging from the conversation.
Method	Grounded theory with an emphasis on procedures for *coding and constant comparative analysis*. May include coding by more than one researcher with an aim to attain a high degree of inter-coder reliability.	Grounded theory with an emphasis on *researcher memoing* and the theoretic sensitivity brought to bear on the texts by the researcher. Assumes that the theory is an interpretive construct generated by the researcher.

TWO DIFFERENT APPROACHES TO A GROUNDED THEORY STUDY OF A GENETIC COUNSELING ISSUE		
Issue	**Post-Positive World View**	**Interpretive World View**
Rationale for multiple "data" sources	Emphasis on triangulation as a technique for promoting convergence toward a set of factors that determines a woman's/couple's decision to accept or reject genetic counseling and prenatal testing. Attempts to establish correspondence between decisions and the factors that determine the decision.	Emphasis on theoretic sampling in order to develop richly divergent exemplars of the existential experience of making a decision about genetic counseling and prenatal testing. Aims to generate as robust portrayal of this existential experience as possible.
Results	A grounded theory that is claimed to serve as a rational-technical model of decision making.	A grounded theory that is claimed as the researcher's heuristic representing counselor stances toward practice.

AFTER WORD

Robin successfully defended her dissertation and subsequently became actively involved in her professional association's deliberations about genetic counseling research. She is working with colleagues to edit *The Oxford Handbook of Genetic Counseling* that will include a chapter with the theory of practice that emerged from her study.

In 2019, Robin received the University of Pittsburgh Chancellor's Distinguished Teaching Award.

Robin's dissertation, *Living with Shadows: Contextualizing the Experience of Being At-Risk and Reaching a Decision about Prenatal Genetic Testing*, can be retrieved from UMI ProQuest Digital Dissertation #AAT 3078844. It is probably most cost effective to work through your university library to obtain the dissertation.

SCENARIO 3.4
A LITERARY CRITICISM OF
A LEAD TEACHER INITIATIVE

COMMENTARY

This Scenario comes from Kathleen M. Ceroni who, at the time of writing her dissertation, was a high school English teacher. We use this Scenario to illustrate several points.

1. The phrase "Promises Made, Promises Broken" in the title conveys the major message of the dissertation. Kathy wrote this title after she completed the study, not as part of her initial proposal. Kathy completed her study in 1995, 15 years after Maria completed the first qualitative dissertation in the school of education. Over the intervening years, those of us in a Dissertation Study Group came to clearer understanding of interpretive inquiry. Having a more evocative, literary title became more acceptable. Pat, who completed her study in 1993 just two years before Kathy, was advised to give a very straightforward, descriptive title. (See title in Scenario 4.2.) This is an example of how discourse communities evolve deeper understandings of a particular area of interest.

2. In claiming literary criticism as her genre, Kathy clearly places herself within an interpretive tradition. This genre fit well with her expertise as a literature teacher.

3. Notice how Kathy embeds information about her logic-of-justification in the abstract.

4. Kathy used the phrase "inner views storied" instead of "interviews," because of the nature of the conversations she had with her study participants. In reviewing the tapes and transcripts of the conversations, it became apparent that she was clarifying her own thinking through the exchanges with others. What she

was portraying in the dissertation was more about her views than an account of others' experiences. This led to a fairly intense discussion during her dissertation defense, but her dissertation held up because she had provided a transparent logic about what the interviews represented.

5. When Kathy uses the term "stance" in her chapter headings, it may seem as though she is referring to her role or perspective. In one sense this is true, but at a deeper level she is signaling ontological shifts as she moves through different phases of the study. For example, in Chapter I she writes in a very personal voice about the context of her study. In Chapter III she steps back from her personal experience and looks dispassionately at formal documents about the lead teacher initiative. What could have seemed like inconsistencies in stance, position, and voice actually strengthened the dissertation by demonstrating "self-conscious method" through an explicit logic of justification for each shift in stance.

Kathy's dissertation can be retrieved from UMI ProQuest Digital Dissertations #AAT 9529234. It is probably most cost effective to work through your university library to obtain the dissertation.

Title: Promises Made, Promises Broken: A Literary Criticism of the Pennsylvania Lead Teacher Experience

Genre: Literary Criticism

Abstract: This study is a personal odyssey of my struggle to come to terms with some of the recurring events and conflicts I have experienced as a teacher. Using the Pennsylvania Lead Teacher Initiative as my context, I examine its roots in teacher development reform discourses and shape an official story of how it was conceived in Pennsylvania.

After interviewing lead teachers and non-lead teachers, I created a series of encounters which I call "inner views storied." Using literary theory (narrative) as a rationale, I create texts that portray the stories of my encounters with my participants in a way that enables the reader to hear our conversations. Since all of the characters in the inner views storied are female, a feminine perspective is present. Interestingly, a disproportionate number of Pennsylvania leader teachers are women.

Using principles of literary and educational criticism, I interpret the texts of the inner views storied, focusing on the surface and embedded meanings in them. I interpret the themes that emerge from a critical theory perspective and convey the appearance/reality dualism within the texts by showing that the Lead Teacher Initiative represents a symbolic effort to "professionalize" teaching, while the lived experience of the teachers involved in the lead teacher programs (mostly women) reveals the effects of proletarianization.

Through this interpretive study, I developed an understanding not only of the ways in which the dominant ideology functions to oppress my class and gender, but also of the ways in which I have acted in complicity with the very forces I have been struggling to combat. The journey has been painful and the wisdom I have come to is a bitter wisdom, yet paradoxically, it has liberated me from the rational, technical mind-set that imbues our culture and has made me available for new beginnings.

Statement of Intent: The intent of this study is to create texts generated within the Pennsylvania Lead Teacher Initiative in order to interpret the surface and embedded meaning within those texts.

Guiding Research Questions:

1. What are some of the texts generated within the Pennsylvania Lead Teacher Initiative?

2. What are surface and embedded themes which emerge from these texts?

3. How are the themes interpreted relative to the appearance/ reality dualism inherent in the texts?

4. How can these interpretations broaden our understanding of the ways in which teachers respond to professional development plans?

Dissertation Format:

Chapter I.   The Promise and the Caution: Teacher Leadership as
              Resource
                        (Stance—Teacher as Researcher)

Chapter II.   The Promise in Perspective: A View of Teacher
              Leadership Incentive Plans
                        (Stance—Researcher as Inquirer)

Chapter III. The Promise Made: The Official Story of the
              Pennsylvania Lead Teacher Initiative
                        (Stance—Researcher as Documenter)

Chapter IV.   Teachers' "Inner Views" of the Pennsylvania Lead
              Teacher Experience
                        (Stance—Researcher as Literary Theorist)

Chapter V.   The Promise Revisited: An Interpretation of the
              Contradictions Embedded in the "Inner Views Storied"
              of the Pennsylvania Lead Teacher Experience
                        (Stance—Researcher as Literary Critic)

Chapter VI.   The Promise Abandoned: The Illusory Nature of
              Teacher Leadership Reform
                        (Stance—Researcher as Teacher)

SCENARIO 3.5
BRINGING FORTH A WORLD:
SPIRITUALITY AS PEDAGOGY

COMMENTARY

Scenario 3.3 illustrated Robin Grub's process for claiming a genre that suited her practice in a field at the interface between physical science and counseling. Her challenge was sorting through different world views of grounded theory. Scenario 3.4 illustrated Kathleen Ceroni's claiming of literary criticism as a genre well-suited to her expertise as a teacher of English literature. This scenario illustrates a different process, not just for claiming a genre, but for creating one—spiritual inquiry. Drawing from multiple life experiences and multiple discourses, Marilyn Llewellyn faced the challenge of providing a logic-of-justification for a genre that's relevance to education might not be readily apparent. Further, she needed a language that would be congruent with the world view embodied in the logic-of-justification. The first two paragraphs in this scenario are Marilyn's abstract. The remainder of this scenario consists of an excerpt drawn from Marilyn's explanation of spiritual inquiry. As you read this scenario, notice the following points.

1. The first sentence indicates not just the intent of the study but also the need to find a language to make the concept of spiritual pedagogy accessible for her intended audience.

2. The field of curriculum comprises several major schools of thought, some of which focus almost exclusively on the practicalities of curriculum design and implementation. The second sentence clearly situates her thinking in the theoretical discourses of curriculum studies, within which there is a discourse about the spiritual nature of education.

3. Recognizing that readers may not immediately relate to the genre of spiritual inquiry, Marilyn includes her logic-of-justification

in Chapter 1 of her "project demonstrating excellence" (her academic institution's equivalent of a dissertation). This is an example of structuring an inquiry report in a way that best lays out the story of the inquiry. In a traditional dissertation, method would be laid out in Chapter 3.

4. Marilyn incorporates the concept of "memoir" as a form of writing that allows her to draw upon lifelong experiences related to themes she is developing. This does not mean she is doing a mixed method study, because she provides a logic-of-justification for memoir within the broader genre of spiritual inquiry.

5. Marilyn's opening sentences in her discussion of method illustrate our point that one does not necessary "find" a genre. Spiritual Inquiry evolved as Marilyn worked through recursive cycles of writing, deliberative conversation, reading, and meditation.

6. Inquiry conventions lay out the sequence of thinking through which the author moves from experience to meaning. Drawing from spiritual discourse traditions, Marilyn articulates her thinking process with the concepts of "kairos," contemplation, meditative writings, and exegesis," which are "faithful" to the subject under study. Her use of "faithful" reflects a sensitivity for language, as it is more appropriate than the term "integrity" which we suggest as one criterion for judging interpretive inquiries.

7. The conventions of interpretation vary among different discourse communities. Kathleen, for example, drew from the discourses of literary criticism for her conventions of interpretation. Marilyn's use of the terms "exegesis" and "hermeneutics" aligns her work with long-standing traditions of interpretation of philosophical, theological, and spiritual texts.

Abstract

This interpretive study explores spirituality, pedagogy, and education. The intent is to articulate an understanding of spirituality as pedagogy and to portray the transformative possibilities in being and learning together in such a way as to make them accessible to other interested educators. The study is intended to further the conversations related to spirituality and education within curriculum theorizing discourses and to contribute to the field of curriculum studies. The following questions guided my study: 1) What brought me to the study of spirituality as pedagogy?; 2) What life events have shaped my spirituality and pedagogy?; 3) How are my spirituality and pedagogy manifested in the "Dealing with Prejudice" pilot curriculum and the experience of co-authoring the *book Dealing with Differences: Taking Action on Class, Race, Gender, and Disability*?; 4) Through a series of meditative writings, how can deeper understandings of spirituality as pedagogy be generated and articulated?; 5) How can essential lessons of spirituality as pedagogy be portrayed? Each question is addressed in a chapter.

Chapter 1 discusses the context of the study and presents the use of spiritual inquiry as a method for engaging in the study. Through narrative portrayals in Chapter 2, life events that have shaped my spirituality and pedagogy are presented as an educational memoir. Chapter 3 is a focused account of one manifestation of "Bringing Forth a World" through the curriculum project Dealing with Prejudice, which culminated in the book *Dealing with Differences*, co-authored with Angele Ellis from our work in an urban high school. Using meditative writings in Chapter 4, I ponder various themes embedded in these life events that reveal deeper understandings of spirituality and pedagogy. Chapter 5 explicates the essential lessons learned and the educational contribution spirituality as pedagogy offers to curriculum studies. New metaphors are needed to shape an understanding of schools as places where growing as a human being is of utmost value and teaching is a human encounter rooted in relationship marked by faith, trust, care, and love. Spirituality as pedagogy is the embodiment of the act of teaching as inseparable from one's very being.

Genre of Spirituality Inquiry—An Excerpt

In this section [of Chapter 1], entitled "Spiritual Inquiry," I describe the inquiry process that I shaped as I engaged in the study. As I entered into this inquiry, a language emerged that allowed me to most clearly express the ways that I engaged in the process. In my study this concept evolved as I engaged in the inquiry process. It became an appropriate way to describe not only what was under study, but also the manner in which I engaged in the study. The inquiry process itself came to embody the spiritual. The Kairos, contemplation, meditative writings and exegesis are the spiritual inquiry. In constructing the inquiry in this way, I was able to draw on a language and create a context for the inquiry that was faithful to what was under study.

While I have not encountered this notion of Spiritual Inquiry as such within educational research, I contend that this type of inquiry is grounded in the educational discourse community of interpretivists whose "works grow out of a hermeneutic orientation based on interpretation and the search for deeper understanding...

CHAPTER 4

Warranting Knowledge Claims and the Issue of Evidence

C reating a conceptually compelling and coherent Scholar-Practitioner Inquiry entails gathering an array of information and using it to construct a persuasive conclusion. To explore what this means we shift from our earlier sports and literature analogies to a legal analogy. In this analogy your role is akin to both a detective searching for evidence and an attorney using the evidence to warrant a particular conclusion.

In the legal system, detectives gather a wide range of evidence, including physical evidence (DNA, finger prints, gun powder residue); eyewitness accounts; expert testimony; hearsay; confessions). Until an attorney puts the evidence together to make a case, it remains an accumulation of bits and pieces of information. To make a case, attorneys follow certain rules, and a judge determines if they have done so. When rules of evidence are violated, the case may be thrown out. Juries are expected to reach a verdict based on whichever case was more persuasive—i.e., better warranted. The peer reviewers mentioned by Shawn Otto are comparable to a jury that determines how credibly evidence has been used to support a case.

In your role as an investigator, you will be searching out information related to the intent of your inquiry.

To do this, it is useful to consider primary, secondary, and tertiary sources of information.

Primary Sources include information you gather directly through observation, interviews, questionnaires, artifacts, etc. In scientific studies, researchers follow conventions to identify a statistically valid sample from which to gather data. In Scholar-Practitioner Inquiry the aim is for thick, rich texts related to the question under study. Different genre have different conventions about gathering primary information.

For example, information gathered through interviews can be used in either scientific or interpretive studies, but the conventions for conducting interviews are different. In a scientific study, an interview protocol is developed and then strictly followed regardless of who is doing the interview. Interview transcripts are then analyzed and coded. Because analysis and coding entail interpretation, often two or more researchers work with the transcripts to minimize bias. (The term "inter-rater reliability is a signal that one is working in a scientific tradition.)

Interpretive interviews are often conducted as conversations loosely guided by a set of questions intended to touch on key points. As the conversation evolves, the interviewer follows up on points of interest, probes for additional details, and offers tentative interpretations to confirm impressions. It is assumed that no two interviewers would gather exactly the same information and the quality of the information would depend greatly on the skills of the interviewer.

Secondary Sources include information that has been gathered and recorded by others in the form of books, journal articles, conference papers, podcasts, personal correspondence, databases, etc. The authors of secondary sources might be considered "expert witnesses." The scholars that we quote throughout this book are examples of secondary sources upon which we draw to elaborate on ideas gained through our professional experiences. These expert witnesses do not prove that our way of thinking is correct or right. Rather, they illustrate that our thinking is aligned with a particular school of thought.

Tertiary Sources include information generated by one author but cited by another. This could be thought of as "hearsay evidence." When it comes to tertiary sources, you will need to decide whether it is necessary to go back to the original source. For example, in Chapter 2 we cited Bent Flyvbjerg's description of "ideal theory." Flyvbjerg had synthesized this description by drawing from two papers written by Herbert Dreyfus. Before quoting Flyvbjerg, we had to decide whether to go back and read Dreyfus' papers. In this case we did not, because the description sufficed as a characterization of scientific knowledge. In contrast, our colleague Micheline Stabile felt a need to go back to an account of Archimedes' use of the word "eureka" to lay a foundation for her use of the term "heuristic inquiry." In part, the decision to rely on Tertiary Information depends on:

- how crucial it is in supporting a point you want to make;
- how crucial the point you want to make is in terms of your overall argument; and
- how thoroughly you want to understand the information.

 The intellectual work of the Exploratory Phase (and continuing throughout your inquiry) is deciding how much credence to place in the information you are gathering. The watch word is "consider the source."

Like a detective following clues, you are likely to come upon promising leads throughout your inquiry. This is an iterative—not linear—process. Your aim is to accumulate a wealth of information to demonstrate that you have engaged in a comprehensive investigation. If you have only a paltry amount of information, you will not be able to construct a compelling conceptual argument. Knowing when to follow the leads and when you have enough information to bring your study to closure is a judgment call, often best made in collaboration with your advisor and/or colleagues. Leads left unfollowed can serve as useful starting points for new studies, and a lifelong agenda of Scholar-Practitioner Inquiry.

The conventions of a genre provide the "rules" by which "evidence" is collected and then how it can be used to warrant knowledge claims. Suppose you want to understand the value of public education in the United States and run across a vehement anti-public school rant on a blog. This could be useful in two ways. First, it might call attention to your own bias that everyone values public education. Second, the blogger represents a particular point of view. You could not use this one piece of information to warrant a general conclusion, but you could use it to illustrate one of many different attitudes towards public education that you unearthed in the course of your investigation.

Students will often ask if it is acceptable to do a "mixed method" study in which numeric and linguistic evidence is provided. Within a Scholar-Practitioner Inquiry, multiple forms and sources of "data" can certainly be "mixed," because different forms of evidence are needed to warrant the different lines of reasoning that comprise an overarching conceptual argument. Suppose, for example, you wanted to explore the reasons that many new teachers leave the field within the first five years of practice. You would need statistics to support the claim that "many new teachers are leaving the field." This would be an important point in making the case for the significance of your study. To understand the reasons teachers are leaving, you might then interview a number of teachers. How you find these individuals to interview, how many you choose to interview, what you ask them, how you record their responses, and how you interpret their responses are all guided by the conventions (the logics) of the genre you are working in. Now you have numeric data (statistics) and linguistic text (interviews), which could be called "mixed data." How you use these two different forms of information to support conclusions is guided by one method—i.e., one genre.

Scholar-Practitioners who are working on a thesis, dissertation, or other form of scholarly product may need to provide an explicit rationale for the type of evidence (information) they have gathered and the conventions they followed in interpreting the information to reach a conclusion. Going back to our legal analogy, when an attorney shouts, "I object," the judge asks for the reasoning behind the presentation of a particular piece of evidence. It is incumbent upon the attorney to provide a rationale within the rules of legal evidence.

Similarly, when the Chinese student's advisor objected and told her, You can't study that," it was incumbent upon the student to offer a rationale for doing so by drawing on the conventions of interpretive inquiry.

This may sound rather adversarial, but it need not be. Under the best of circumstances, a student's advisor and committee help to guide the inquiry so it yields well-warranted conclusions. Also, in the best of circumstances, advisors and committee members may be learning along with the student. This is a point that Scholar-Practitioners may not realize. One of the joys of working with bright and dedicated students is an opportunity for faculty to learn about ideas they do not have time to pursue.

The type of evidence needed to warrant the knowledge claims will be determined by the intent and guiding questions of each inquiry. Therefore, it is difficult to offer general guidelines. Instead, we provide the following two scenarios to illustrate the types of information gathered by Scholar-Practitioners who are studying their practice.

SCENARIO 4.2
WARRANTING INTERPRETIVE
KNOWLEDGE CLAIMS

COMMENTARY

Scenario1.2 introduced Pat McMahon's troubling moment with a former student. At the heart of that moment was a pedagogical issue which became the focus for her dissertation. Pat situated her study in her teaching of English composition during one semester at a community college. We use this Scenario to illustrate a number of points.

1. Pat could have claimed "case study" as her genre with a title like "A Case Study of a College Composition Class." Pat, however, thinks in narrative. She often writes fictive accounts to capture troubling moments.[1] In a sense, this is her form of journaling. So it was quite logical for Pat to claim narrative as her genre.

2. The *practice context* for her study was the composition classes she taught at a community college. One of her logics was the decision to study her classes for an entire semester. This would allow her to gather thick, rich information. We mention this because we have seen studies where teachers look at a single lesson or two and then make claims about the value of the lesson. Rarely have these "snap shots" yielded compelling insights.

3. The *conceptual context* of her study was shaped by three major concepts. For some time she had been interested in the use of portfolios for pedagogical purposes. She had also been interested in the nature of reflection and how reflection informs learning. Her third interest was narrative writing as a process for meaning making. Notice how these concepts are incorporated into the title

---

1 Patricia L. McMahon, "From Angst to Story to Research Text: The Role of Arts-based Educational Research in Teacher Inquiry," *Journal of Curriculum Theorizing* 16, no1 (2000): 125-145.

of her dissertation, thereby setting the conceptual parameters of her study.

4. Notice the phrase "three levels of reflection." This points to her intention to gather "thick texts." One text would be her teacher journal in which she would capture her own reflections. A second set of texts would be the portfolios prepared by the students, which would capture their reflections. The third form of text was the discourse between her students and her, which would capture how they reflected together on the students' work.

5. Discourse in the form of class conversation is illusive. Creating a stable record of that would be difficult. (In fact, some inquirers video record classes to create a stable record.) Pat decided to use her email exchanges with students as the stable record of their mutual reflections. This is an example of a logic-of-justification; it is a rationale for using emails as a useful primary source of information.

6. Because the term "explanation" has connotations of scientific explanatory theory, Pat uses the term "explicate" in the statements of intent. Explication has the connotation of providing detailed descriptions that illuminate a phenomenon without the implication of causal explanation.

7. As you read through the Abstract, notice the structure of Pat's dissertation. Rather than following the formatting conventions of a scientific report, she develops a structure that better lays out each step of her inquiry.

8. Notice how Pat's discussion of each guiding question describes what she did and the reasoning behind each approach.

9. One of the challenges of Scholar-Practitioner Inquiry is crafting what we call "experiential text." It would be logistically impossible for Pat to include 65 portfolios in the dissertation. Few people would want to read them and, even if they did, what would they make of them? The challenge is preserving the richness of experience while portraying it in a compelling and informative way. If you recall the physician's negative reaction to

the earthquake study, it is very likely that the researchers did not provide a compelling portrayal of the survivors' experience. They extracted a generalization that was so broad, it was meaningless.

10. Pat's dissertation also illustrates the creative crux of interpretive inquiry. Given the wealth of primary and secondary information she has gathered, how does she make sense of it and offer useful insights? The four types of reflective responses she mentions are an example of a heuristic. It is also an example of the meaning-making inherent in interpretive inquiry. Another person looking at the same texts might have conceptualized the nature of the students' reflection in an entirely different way. We mentioned "aesthetics" as one criteria for judging interpretive inquiries. Consider how an artist working within the impressionist tradition would produce a very different painting from one working in the cubist or realist traditions. Each is following the conventions of a particular tradition to convey what they see in the landscape. This is also the case in interpretive inquiry where the portrayal is an expression of the author's understanding.

Title: A Narrative Study of Three Levels of Reflection in a College Composition Class: Teacher Journal, Student Portfolios, Teacher-Student Discourse.

Inquiry Genre: Personal Narrative

Statement of Intent: The intent of my research is to explicate the concept of teacher reflective practice through a teacher journal. I will also explicate the concept of reflection in writing portfolios through a narrative study of composition students' portfolio entries and through teacher-student portfolio discourse.

Abstract: This is a narrative study which focuses on the struggles of a composition teacher wishing to create a more personally meaningful learning experience for students and teacher alike. In Chapter I, I introduce my desire to involve students more rigorously in their own writing process and in the life of the class. In Chapter II, I begin to think about reflection in the composition curriculum and devise an educational encounter to engage my students in the process of reflection.

The centerpiece of this curriculum is the requirement of a writing portfolio, for which I provide no specific guidelines or model. Purposely problematizing the learning experience, I ask my students to capture their thinking both in the form of the reflective content of their portfolio and in negotiating for themselves a reflective procedure which allows them to create the structure of the portfolio itself.

Chapter III, my reflective journal, is the story of what occurs in the classroom as a result of this task. Here I explain what transpires during the course of one semester when students are asked to construct knowledge for themselves, and I describe our work as a discourse community as we attempt to understand how knowledge is made and what it means to reflect.

In Chapter IV, I am faced with the task of analyzing 65 student portfolios in order to reach conclusions about the nature of reflection exhibited within them. Struggling to envision a conceptual framework to capture the range of material before me, I realize I am working to make meaning, trusting the same inductive process in which I had placed my students. Eventually, I see my students' writing as their means of making sense of the portfolio experience itself.

Four categories of response to the portfolio emerge: "Searching for Boundaries," "Finding a Voice," "Pursuing Connections," "Making Discoveries." I describe each mode of Interpretation in Chapter V, where I present individual portrayals of students' reflection as it is represented in their writing and in their discourse.

Guiding Research Questions and Research Procedures: This dissertation looks at what occurs when the reflective writing portfolio becomes the cornerstone of a community college English Composition 101 curriculum. For the purpose of this study, I have generated 5 guiding questions.

1. What is the story of the educational encounter in a community college composition class?

2. What happens when the writing teacher reflects on her own practice?

These questions are addressed in the form of my own reflective journal, which I kept throughout the semester (15 weeks) in order

to capture evidence of my reflective processes. In it I describe my
rationale and structure for the English Composition 101 curriculum,
and I explain how I shaped the educative events at the outset of the 15-
week course. I continuously reflect on my own pedagogy as a way of
articulating my understanding of the learning experience as it unfolds.
Because I wish to present my thinking in its authentic journal form, that
part of this study, Chapter III, "My Story of the Educational Encounter:
A Teacher Reflects on Her Practice,' is single-spaced.

1. How does a writing teacher deal with a large number of writing
   portfolios?

In this section, I describe my thoughts and feelings as I attempt
to reach conclusions about the nature of reflection exhibited in the 65
student portfolios. I explain the stages of my inductive search to create
a conceptual framework which captures the various forms of students'
reflective work. I also include my reflection on theory as a means of
making sense of my experience. This section of the study, Chapter IV,
is entitled, "Facing Sixty-Five Portfolios: Reflection Relating Theory
to Practice.

1. What is the nature of reflective writing as exhibited in the
   portfolios of students? and

2. What is the nature of the discourse between students and teacher
   about the students' reflective writing?

These questions are addressed in Chapter V, "A Conceptual
Framework by which to Consider Portfolio Reflection and Teacher-
Student Discourse." This chapter contains excerpts of reflective work
from the student portfolios as well as the ongoing discourse that
occurred between students and teacher when students are encouraged
to use their writing as a means for reflection. The conceptual framework
comprises four categories, and in each of these categories, I present
individual student portrayals. These portrayals allow me to capture the
students' portfolio content and interpret how this content exemplifies
the reflective characteristics of its category. At the same time, these
portrayals also capture the nature of the discourse between students and
teacher. For evidence of this discourse, I refer to correspondence in the

form of notes between my students and me as well as moments from my own taped reactions to teacher-student conferences.

AFTER WORD

As a Scholar-Practitioner, Pat has continued to incorporate into her pedagogy the lessons she learned through her dissertation inquiry. She has co-created two graduate programs and numerous courses built around the pedagogical concept of "contrived ambiguity." This concept lies at the heart of her on-going, professional learning agenda.

Her dissertation can be accessed through UMI Proquest Digital Dissertation # ATT 9329582. It is probably most cost effective to work through your university library to obtain the dissertation.

SCENARIO 4.3
WARRANTING INTERPRETIVE
KNOWLEDGE CLAIMS

COMMENTARY

Scenario1.3 introduced Micheline Stabile's troubling moment captured in her "Timmy Story." Decades later, this moment led to her study of educational inclusion as a policy mandate. We use this Scenario to illustrate a number of points.

1. The term "problematizing" in the title signals the form of knowledge generated through the study. Her field of special education often frames issues within a medical, problem-solving model which aims to correct social or learning deficits. Micheline's educational philosophy aligns her with a different school of thought about special education. By using the concept of "problematics" rather than "problems," she signals an intention to lay out the complexities inherent in an educational phenomenon and avoid overly simplistic either/or thinking.

2. Micheline Stabile claims the genre of "practice-based heuristic inquiry." She debated for some time about using the term "practice-based" to qualify "heuristic inquiry." As she reviewed the discourses on heuristic inquiry, she was uncomfortable with the intensely introspective and psychological nature of many dissertations that fell within that genre. Yet, she felt an affinity for the meaning-making process of heuristic inquiry. Her hesitancy about modifying heuristic inquiry stemmed from uncertainty of "Who am I to reframe the nature of this genre?" In the end, two perspectives persuaded her to take this step. One was a reminder that, as a Scholar-Practitioner, she had a right to add her perspective to the discourses on heuristic inquiry. The other was her own growing conviction that her title should explicitly indicate the practice-oriented nature of her study. In

the body of her proposal, Micheline explained her view of the relationship between "practice-based" and "heuristic inquiry" thereby providing an explicit logic-of-justification for her inquiry process.

3. If you recall, we mentioned Micheline's need to go back to original sources for the concept of "heuristics." Although she could not read the original Greek, she could use secondary sources that explicate the concept instead of relying on tertiary sources that merely alluded to the concept as though everyone understood its origins. In part Micheline was motivated by a need to provide a starting point to justify her adaptation of the method. It is unlikely that Micheline's committee would have expected or needed that foundation, but Micheline's need for deep learning would not be satisfied with a less thorough understanding.

4. The introductory section of Micheline's dissertation is presented in Scenario 1.3. In reviewing that Scenario, notice the verbal and conceptual economy with which she frames the study. In two relatively short paragraphs, she places the current inquiry within a personal context that spans 25 years of professional growth and intellectual development. She conveys not only her initial biases, but also how these preconceptions were shaken—moving her to a more deliberative stance toward the dissertation. Also woven into this background is information about her professional roles and her perspective on regular and special education. From this personal opening, Micheline then provides a more formal frame for the study by linking her concerns to three discourses:

   Special Education: Introductory Perspectives

   Educational Inclusion: Introductory Perspectives

   A World Divided: Perspectives of an Educational Administrator

5. See how the concepts of problematizing and educational inclusion are carried forward from the title into the intent. The consistency of language and wording begin to create a sense of conceptual

coherence. When students vary the wording in the title and intent, sometimes it seems inadvertent, as though little thought has been given to the relationship between these two facets of the study. In other cases, the variations seem more deliberate—an attempt to make the writing "interesting" by changing words or sentence structure. We encourage students to be more straightforward, echoing key concepts from the title in the statement of intent.

1. The purpose or "So what?" of the study is made explicit. Embedded in the purpose are the prospective audiences for the study as well—educational policymakers and administrators.

2. Both the title and intent convey Micheline's position in relation to her study: that is, educational inclusion is viewed too simplistically and "needs to be" problematized. Rather than trying to pretend or obscure this position, she makes it explicit and subsequently provides a rationale for her position. One reason that Micheline could take this approach is the thoroughness with which she had immersed herself in the formal discourses on educational inclusion in her comprehensive examination and the open-minded stance she exhibited when describing perspectives she encountered in her practice setting.

3. Notice the conciseness with which so much information is communicated—the "what," "how," and "so what?" of the inquiry as well as Micheline's position toward the phenomenon under study, the discourses to which the study will contribute, and the audiences who are likely to find the results of her study of interest/use. Although each of these points requires elaboration, the conceptual richness of the title and statement of intent convey the impression of someone who is in command of her inquiry process.

4. Practice-based heuristic inquiry" indicates the inquiry genre. When "problematizing" and "heuristic" are considered together, they foreshadow the nature of the portrayal that Micheline aims to generate—a heuristic representation of the problematic aspects of educational inclusion.

Dissertation Title: A Call to Conscience: Problematizing Educational Inclusion
Inquiry Genre: Practice-based Heuristic
Introduction of the Study: See Scenario 1.3
Statement of Intent: The intent of my study is to "problematize" the concept of educational inclusion for the purpose of informing educational policy and administrative practice.
Guiding Research questions and Research Procedures

COMMENTARY (CONTINUED)

Drawing from discourses on heuristics dating back to Archimedes, Micheline lays out key phases of her inquiry process in the form of guiding research questions. Each of the phrases set off in quotation marks (engagement, immersion, acquisition, etc.) relates to a specific facet of heuristic inquiry. Recognizing that these concepts might not be familiar to readers, Micheline provided a thumbnail sketch of the heuristic inquiry process as part of her introduction. Later, in the Procedures section of the proposal, she returned to these concepts and explained in more detail how she carried out these processes.

1. What is the nature of my "initial engagement" with the concept of educational inclusion?

2. What processes can I use to accomplish the intent of my study?

3. How do I move from initial engagement to "immersion" and "acquisition" through the discourses related to educational inclusion found in selected literature?

4. How do I move from "immersion" and "acquisition" within the literature to "immersion" through the discourse that is part of my administrative practice?

5. How do I portray the problematic nature of educational inclusion that I have come to "realize" through the processes of immersion and acquisition?

6. What heuristic can be "creatively synthesized" to inform educational policy and administrative practice regarding educational inclusion?

AFTER WORD

Micheline won the outstanding dissertation award given by her university's school of education. Her study was clearly an interpretive inquiry—a stark departure from the science-like studies that for decades had been the default dissertation form in the school's department of administrative studies. The faculty member who chaired the awards committee was a well-regarded researcher who worked in a scientific tradition. Yet, he commented, "A rigorous study is a rigorous study, regardless of tradition." This offers an instructive contrast to the physician's condemnation of the earthquake study. In that case, either the study itself was poorly conceived or the portrayal of it failed to convey the rigor of the inquiry.

Micheline also received the 2000 Mary Catherine Ellwein Outstanding Dissertation Award of Division D and the Qualitative Special Interest Group of the American Education Research Association.

Micheline's award winning dissertation can be accessed at UMI Proquest Digital Dissertations # AAT 9928088. It is probably most cost effective to work through your university library to obtain the dissertation.

SECTION 2

Developing My Scholar-Practitioner Inquiry Profile

> *"The important thing is to not stop questioning.
> Curiosity has its own reason for existing."*
> – ALBERT EINSTEIN

> *"Funny how 'question' contains the word
> 'quest' inside it, as though any small question
> asked is a journey through briars."*
> – CATHERYNNE M. VALENTE

> *"A real education includes learning that you don't
> know certain things (a lot of things). Instead of looking
> in at the knowledge you do have, you learn to look out
> at the knowledge you don't have. To do this, you have
> to let go of some hubris; you have to accept that you
> don't know what you don't know. Learning what you
> don't know is just a matter of looking at the frontiers
> of your knowledge and wondering what is out there
> beyond the border. It's about asking why."*
> – STEVEN SLOMAN & PHILIP FERNBACH
> *The Knowledge Illusion: Why We Never Think Alone*

CHAPTER 5

Developing a Practice Context for Inquiry

Who Am I as a Practitioner?

What Is the Nature of My Practice?

Purpose

Scholar-Practitioner inquiries typically begin with an issue, question, problem, or dilemma embedded within contexts of practice. What you see and deal with is shaped by your role and the setting in which you work. For example, teachers may see an issue like educational inclusion one way, principals another way, and superintendents a third way. Or, the head of an independent private school may see her job differently than a principal in a large urban public school. Community-based educators working in museums or social support non-profits will have issues that differ from those working in higher education. The following prompts invite you to brainstorm possibilities for situating an inquiry in your role and setting.

Reflective Prompts

Role and Setting

What is your current professional role and in what setting is that role embedded? For example, roles might be teacher, principal, superintendent, curriculum specialist, instructional supervisor, faculty member, academic dean, museum educator. Settings might be public or private schools, elementary or secondary schools, a technical school, a college or university, a museum, hospital, rehabilitation center, or library.

Have you had other roles in the past? For example, have you been a pre-school teacher and then moved to elementary school? Have you been a school superintendent who is now teaching in a university program? Were you a classroom history teacher who became the chair of your district's social studies department?

Are you preparing to move into another role or the same role but in a different setting? Are you, for example, a teacher enrolled in an administrative leadership program or a principal aiming to become a superintendent? Do you work in an affluent suburban school but want to change to an urban school; or vice versa? Have you been a religious education teacher at your church and want to become a high school English teacher?

The point is that many practitioners have experience with a number of roles and settings. Think broadly, making notes about your current and past roles and roles to which you aspire. Consider both formal and informal roles in which you engaged with others in a process of teaching and learning.

Professional Organizations

Typically, the role and setting that come most immediately to mind is that associated with one's work. But there is another context that can shape who you are as a scholar-practitioner—the professional organizations to which you belong. In this section, record information about your role within such organizations.

To what organizations do you belong—e.g., a union, a professional association, a special interest group?

What is your role—e.g., member, committee member or chair, officer?

What is the nature of your involvement—e.g., extensive, marginal, occasional?

Communities of Practice

Communities of practice are often more amorphous than formally organized professional organizations. Examples include committees, task forces, special project teams, commissions, groups of professional colleagues who gather routinely to share experiences.

To what communities of practice do you belong?
What is the nature of your involvement?
What is meaningful to you about these communities?

Reflective Interlude

As you review the notes on your context of practice, consider from what perspective you want to conduct your inquiry. For example, if you have been a teacher but are now studying to be a principal or superintendent, which of these professional roles will shape your inquiry, the way you will ultimately write it, and the professional community that will be most interested in what you have to say? Or, if you have been both a regular education and special education teacher, will one or both roles shape your inquiry? Perhaps you want to draw from multiple roles for your inquiry—essentially offering multiple perspectives on whatever issue you study. As you begin to focus more specifically on an inquiry topic, clarify the practice setting in which it is embedded and the position from which you will be writing.

Keep in mind that the role and setting help to define which communities of practice will be most interested in the results of your inquiry. As you work on your study, imagine the audience to whom you will be writing.

CHAPTER 6

Capturing Moments of Practice

What are troubling aspects of my practice?

*In what troubling "moment(s)"
will I embed my inquiry?*

Purpose

If you are enrolled in a Master's or doctoral program, you may have been advised to find a problem to study. This may leave you wondering: Where do I begin to look? Where do these problems lurk? How will I recognize a problem? Our answer to these questions is to look within yourself and your practice.

Caring and thoughtful practitioners often experience "troubling moments," experiences that have not gone as well as they had hoped. Sometimes these moments occur in a flash; others may continue for an extended period of time. The Reflective Prompts in this chapter encourage you to capture such moments so you can begin to reflect on them as potential topics for study.

Somewhat arbitrarily we clustered the following questions under the headings of "Situations That Trouble Me," "Issues That Puzzle Me," and "Questions That Haunt Me." Our aim is to provide an array of prompts, some of which may be more compelling to you than others. Use the prompts as catalysts for reflection and don't worry about categorizing emerging ideas under specific headings.

It is worth noting that some moments linger in our memories in full-blown detail. Others may surface as little more than a fleeting image. Sometimes they come in the form of a dream. However clear or vague they may be, the important work for a Scholar-Practitioner Inquiry is to capture these recollections so you can examine them more closely.

Reflective Prompts

Situations That Trouble Me

Have you found yourself in situations that are troubling? Perhaps an instructional plan went awry. Perhaps a meeting did not go as well as you had hoped. Perhaps at a professional conference everyone seemed to "be on the same page," but that "page" didn't make much sense to you. Perhaps you've been advocating for a particular change, but your efforts meet with resistance. Such situations can be unsettling, frustrating, and confusing. They can also be a valuable source of questions to study. Keeping track of such situations entails making notes about:

- What happened?
- When did it happen?
- Who was involved?
- What was at stake?
- Was there a particular turning point when the situation went awry?
- What were you feeling at the time?
- What triggered those feelings?

Issues That Puzzle Me

Issues that recur with alarming frequency are another potential source of ideas for your study. For example, how often do you see a newscast, a Tweet, a newspaper headline with breaking news about the latest school shooting, the gap in achievement scores, a new set of standards, a new policy or regulation and think, "Oh no, not again?" Are you perplexed by issues that seem intractable? No matter what interventions are tried to deal with the issue, finding a "fix" remains elusive. If you ponder why such issues persist, make notes about them.

List your questions. Imagine you had the power to fix them; what would you do? As you brainstorm, consider the difference between issues, problems, and dilemmas.

Questions That Haunt Me

Here are two examples of haunting questions. One example came from a pre-school teacher who was accused by an irate parent of "having my son play all day; you're not helping him learn anything; you're setting him up for failure." She was haunted by the inadequacy of her response to this parent, her inability to articulate the importance of play in early childhood learning. This incident led to the shaping of her Master's thesis. The other example came from a substitute teacher who had prepared a lesson to engage students in thinking about science. Her supervisor told her that the students were not capable of entering into the activities she had planned, and they needed to read the book. Taking a deep breath, the substitute teacher began to ask the students to take turns reading. Again, she was interrupted and told that she had to read the book to the students. This experience led her to think about the role, responsibilities, and authority of substitute teachers, a subject that could very well have been an excellent scholar-practitioner inquiry.

Reflect on moments that have troubled you, moments that periodically nag at you. Do you ruminate on what you could have done differently; what you could have said; why the situation went awry? Do you sometimes wonder "If I had known then what I know now, would that have made things better?" What situations and questions come to mind?

Reflective Interlude

Periodically revisit the notes you've made in response to the Reflective Prompts in this chapter. Flag the notes that are most compelling. Look for items that overlap. During initial brainstorming, you may be torn between several different "troubles." Give yourself time to decide which direction is most compelling. Talk with others and take their responses into considerations. *Scenario 6.1* illustrates one student's early musings about potential topics.

If you had to decide on a topic for your thesis or dissertation today, which item(s) would you be most interested in studying? Finish the following sentence. What I really want to understand is… *Scenario 6.2* illustrates one student's early brainstorming about questions she was pondering.

Eventually, as you begin to refine your thinking, a "defining moment" will begin to emerge. It is "defining" in the sense that it defines the beginning of your thinking about a troubling aspect of practice, and it defines the start of your inquiry. In other words, if you are conducting a Scholar-Practitioner Inquiry, you will need a brief description of that moment to set the context for your study. Review *Scenarios 1.1, 1.2, and 1.3* for examples of such descriptions.

A clear and compelling description of your troubling moment contributes to the verisimilitude of your Inquiry. Often it takes several drafts to craft a good description. Practice writing one or more moments; share the drafts with others; take their reactions into account as you refine the description. Like GoldiLocks and the Three Bears, you don't want too many details or too few; you want it to be just right.

SCENARIO 6.1
TORN BETWEEN TOPICS

COMMENTARY

During an introductory course on qualitative research, Wendy Milne, an art teacher in a semi-rural school district, wrote the following reflection. As you read her thoughts, notice Wendy's dual focus. On one hand, there is a fairly narrow focus on a particular instructional technique—the use of reflection sheets with elementary school students. With this focus, Wendy runs the risk of cheerleading for a particular instructional technique. On the other hand, she has a rather grandiose desire to challenge the educational establishment's perceived devaluing of art. Such widely divergent possibilities often appear in students' early writings. The issue is moving beyond these vaguely formed notions to a viable study.

Embedded in Wendy's writing are two key phrases that suggest avenues for further deliberation. At the end of the first paragraph, Wendy makes a tentative connection between the reflection she expects of her students and her weakness for this type of thinking. This raises the possibility of connecting her ideas to the educational discourses on teacher reflection. At the end of the second paragraph, Wendy expresses misgivings about sounding like a complainer. This provides an entry point for discussing two important issues in Scholar-Practitioner Inquiry—stance and voice. It also hints at potential bodies of discourse that might provide insights into the significance of the study—namely, the discourses on aesthetic knowing and rationales for art education. Through on-going deliberation, Wendy eventually came to the concept of "reflective artmaking" which served as the centerpiece of her study which won the American Research Education Association's Mary Catherine Ellwein Outstanding Qualitative Dissertation Award.[1]

---

1   As an art teacher and artist, Wendy relies heavily on visual images to express her thinking. To see an example of how she incorporated her reflective sketches into her writing see Wendy

Currently, I have two topics which I am interested in researching....
The first topic deals with a process which I believe is quite valuable
to children in the art room. I call this process reflection sheets. These
reflection sheets have taken on many forms but are usually used at
the end of a project or unit, and their purpose is to get the students
to evaluate and reflect upon their work in the hope that they will
recall their strengths and weaknesses when they begin a new project.
Although many art teachers provide reflection sheets to their students,
I believe mine have a unique form. Also, those art teachers that do
provide reflection sheets often only do so at the middle school or high
school level. Another advantage I have in using the reflection sheets is
that I keep them from year to year, and I keep the artwork throughout
the school year. This enables me to see the growth in their drawings as
well as their growth in the reflection sheets. Possibly, I feel the need
to research this topic since I find that my personal weakness lies in
reflecting upon a project which I have completed.

My second topic is the one that I feel most strongly about. It goes
something like this. Over the past ten years the role of the art teacher
has drastically changed but the perception of the art teacher has not.
The only people that I see who value art as an equally important subject
are my students. My teaching peers, administrators and parents have
verbally stated this view of unimportance or somehow have silently
implied that my field is less than important. I find that I frequently
express frustration over this lack of respect. However, I am concerned
that if I choose this topic it will just sound as if I'm complaining.

A. Milne, "Imagining Reflective Artmaking: Claiming Self as Artist-Teacher-Researcher,"
Noreen B. Garman and Maria Piantanida, eds., *The Authority to Imagine: The Struggle toward
Representation in Dissertation Writing* (Pittsburgh: Learning Moments Press, 2018): 173-
185. Wendy won the Mary Catherine Ellwein Outstanding Dissertation Award for qualitative
inquiry. Her dissertation, *Reflective Artmaking: Implications for Art Education*, can be
retrieved from UMI ProQuest Digital Dissertation AAT 9974457. It is probably most cost
effective to work through your university library to obtain the dissertation.

SCENARIO 6.2
FROM A LAUNDRY LIST OF
QUESTIONS TO A STUDY

COMMENTARY

The questions listed below were generated by Lynn A. Richards, an elementary school teacher in a suburban school district. Notice how many of the questions are framed to yield a yes/no answer. This indicates that more work is needed, because interpretive inquiries do not aim for such definitive conclusions. Also notice that the questions suggest a variety of potential avenues for a study. Questions 1, 3 and 13, for example, tend to have a more psychological thrust, looking for cause-and-effect relationships between creative drama as an instructional intervention and self-esteem, empathy, and student learning. Some questions (e.g., 4 and 7) focus more specifically on student acquisition of literacy and oral language skills. Still others (e.g., 1, 6, 8, 9, 10, 12) are more pedagogically oriented but tend to be framed in terms of cause and effect. When Lynn revised this list a few weeks later, most of the questions remained the same except for a few minor changes in wording. Of significance, however, was the following question that Lynn added to the list—"What happens when a teacher facilitates creative drama activities in the classroom?" This additional question, when coupled with Question 14, eventually led to the central focus of Lynn's study and helped her to recraft the statement of intent and final guiding research questions.

1. How does creative drama contribute to a cooperative classroom climate? Do consistent, warm and "nonjudgmental" school experiences impact on self-esteem?

2. Does creative drama help students to connect specific content knowledge to real-world experiences?

3. Does creative drama promote a young child's awareness of and empathy with others. Can drama activities expedite "de-centering"?

4. Do creative drama activities/learnings transform into emerging literacy and emergent student writing?

5. Can "gaps" in readers' prior knowledge be instantiated through participation in creative drama activities? Do "active classrooms develop active readers?" (or learners?)

6. How can holistic learning be facilitated by the creative drama process? How does creative drama address Eisner's idea of "broadening educational equity" for all students?

7. What effect does participation in creative drama activities have on oral language development?

8. Does creative drama significantly promote student-to-student interactions as opposed to traditional "teacher asks and one student responds" classroom dialogue?

9. How does the role of the teacher adjust as the structure of drama in the classroom leads from diminished teacher direction to more loosely structure, child-developed activities?

10. How does the leader's ability to ask searching, skillful, and reflective questions contribute to the quality of drama/learning experiences of the children?

11. What are the understandings of the participants involved in the drama experiences? How does the debriefing process make visible the child's perceptions of the teacher's intended plan/ objectives of the lesson? What reciprocal learning processes (student to teacher as well as teacher to student) are facilitated?

12. What feature of the classroom setting (physical, social, temporal, and spatial) are changed as the children are engaged in creative drama experiences? How are the interactions/behaviors of the participants instigated, sustained, and developed?

13. Do intermediate-aged school children and primary-aged elementary school children exhibit different patterns of learning

in their creative drama participation? Is drama applicable across age levels in all instructional applications? Are some content areas more "teachable" for different drama stages and cognitive ages?

14. What are the implications for the elementary classroom practitioner and/or the teacher educator?

COMMENTARY (CONTINUED)

From the questions listed above, Lynn eventually crafted a narrative study of her pedagogical use of creative dramatics in her classroom.

The second paragraph of Lynn's abstract summarizes the various forms of information she gathered to fulfill the intent of the study and the purposes served by the information. The dissertation chapter outline illustrates how Lynn organized her information to support different aspects of the inquiry.

The third paragraph summarizes the conceptual results of the study.

It's important to note that this concise description of the study was written at the end of the inquiry process. Until then, Lynn was still working through the details and structure. Abstracts tend to be Metacognitive Reflections on the entire inquiry process.

Lynn's dissertation, *Pictures in Our Minds*, can be accessed through UMI ProQuest Digital Dissertation #ATT 9637875. It is probably most cost effective to work through your university library to obtain the dissertation.

Dissertation Title: Pictures in Our Minds: A Narrative Study of the Incorporation of Creative Dramatics as Pedagogy in Elementary Classroom Content Areas

Statement of Intent: The intent of this research is to delineate creative dramatics as pedagogy. This narrative study also investigates how primary school children's content area learning is shaped by the classroom drama process.

Guiding Research Questions:

1. How can creative drama be construed as pedagogy?

2. What happens when a teacher uses drama as pedagogy in an elementary classroom?

3. How are the narratives of the classroom interpreted?

4. What are the pedagogical implications of using creative drama in the elementary classroom?

Abstract: This narrative study represents one elementary educator's search for pedagogical insight. I begin by describing my initial professional orientation toward the field of creative dramatics and my interest in how an elementary classroom could be infused with drama activities across the curriculum. Throughout the study, I connected my personal experiences with the thoughts of other researchers, drama theorists, teachers, and especially with the voices of my own students.

Over a span of six months, I document my second-grade classroom practices through the multiple lenses of teacher journal, lesson plans, and audio/videotapes. I also include those modes of student response which informed my thinking: learning logs, essay writings, journals, audio/videotape transcriptions and drama debriefing field notes. Through narrative vignettes, I explore the implicit contradictions in the varied roles and generic responsibility of the elementary classroom teacher, especially in how the boundaries of Teacher and Student become blurred as drama activities are incorporated into each content area. My examination of the ongoing drama activities as debriefings are further guided by two questions: "What are my intentions as teacher?" and "What are the children's perceptions?"

Within this instructional context, I portray how my pedagogic philosophies, the connections between home and school life, and daily classroom events collide with, meld into, and transform the prescribed language arts, social studies, mathematics, and science curricula. I then synthesize these portrayals into broader pedagogic contexts by construing drama as four analogies: "Drama as Knowing," "Drama as Discourse," "Drama as Narrative," and "Drama as Synectics." These categories are described through classroom examples of the children's diverse ways of making meaning, extended student-to-student discussions, contextualization of drama experiences through shared narrative discourse, Teacher-Student sharing of role and life stage synergy, and how creative drama is embedded within the teaching-learning process. I conclude this study with some broad observations for other elementary educators who are committed to incorporating drama as pedagogy within their own classroom life.

Chapter I: Introduction
              Intent of the Study
              Guiding Questions
              Importance of the Study

Chapter II: Drama Definitions, A Selected Review of the Literature
              Definitions of Drama in Education
              Drama as Subject and as Process
              Types of Educational Drama
              Classroom Drama Situated in Educational Context

Chapter III: Drama Data, The Study Process
              Narrative Inquiry
              Description of the School Setting
              The Children
              Duration of the Study
              The Data Collection Process
              Data Analysis Procedures
              The Narrative Genre of the Study

Chapter IV: Drama Depictions, The Narratives of Our Classroom
              Drama and Pedagogic Practice
              A Dramatic Picture
              Dramatic Teacher Performance
              The Drama of Daily Classroom Routines

AFTER WORD

Reading dissertations is not generally considered a leisurely past-time. Pamela Krakowski (whose study we discuss in Scenario 7.1) expresses her reluctance for such reading, a reluctance probably shared by many practitioners:

Until the second night of a qualitative research course, I had never read a dissertation. I imagined those foreboding black-bound books were boring, full of hard-to-decipher statistics, with little relevance to classroom practice.

Pam goes on to recount how she came to question her stereotypes of dissertations.

I picked up one of the dissertations at the end of class and read the title: *Pictures in Our Minds: A*

Narrative Study of Creative Dramatics as Pedagogy in Elementary Classroom Content Areas. It intrigued me, so I borrowed it.

That night, instead of watching television, I sat down to read the dissertation. I found I could not put it down. It read like a story and was full of accounts I could relate to as a teacher. I kept asking, "Are you really allowed to do this?" I couldn't believe that a teacher was allowed to write about her own teaching, in her own context, much less in narrative form.

Pam's comment points to the aesthetic quality of well-crafted interpretive inquiry. Not all dissertations offer compelling reading. Nor are all dissertations examples of high quality studies. That said, it is useful to seek out and read dissertations that can inform (even inspire) your own work. We have included citations for the dissertations from which the *Scenarios* have been drawn. To find other examples of meritorious dissertations, ask your advisor for recommendations. Also look at recipients of the distinguished dissertations awards given by the American Education Research Association (aera.net).

CHAPTER 7

Developing a Conceptual Context for Inquiry

*What do I already know about
matters that trouble me?*

*How has my prior learning prepared
me to embark on a study?*

Purpose

Chapters 5 and 6 prompted you to reflect on your *practice context* and identify troubling moments. Embedded in those moments are potential avenues for inquiry. Now it is time to consider the knowledge you already bring to bear on the events that are troubling you. As you think about the following prompts, keep in mind Shawn Otto's comment that "both [art and science] are driven forward by an intensely disciplined focus." We take "disciplined focus" to have two connotations. One is the idea of careful, rigorous, persistent attention to the matter under study. This is in contrast to casual, occasional, or haphazard attention.

The second connotation is the idea that inquiry is guided by conventions within disciplines. This is especially important for educational research because we, as a profession, draw from many disciplines. For example, psychology has guided much research into the nature of learning. Sociology and anthropology have guided research into schools as social institutions. Curriculum scholars have drawn from philosophy, history, and the arts.

When you entered the world of higher education, you entered a world of ideas. Your choice of program and degree aligned you with a particular discipline or field of study. One aim of academic programs is to help newcomers assimilate the ways in which members of a field or discipline think about:

- The nature of knowledge,
- The nature of intellectual problems worth studying,
- The nature of research that is valued, and
- The theoretical foundations of the field/discipline.

The prompts below encourage you to reflect on disciplined fields of study that have been shaping the way you think about yourself, your world of practice, and the nature of your professional work. These constitute the intellectual background you bring to an inquiry and begin to shape the *conceptual context* for your study.

Reflective Prompts

Formal Field(s) of Study

What was your undergraduate major and minor?

What have you studied (or are studying) at the graduate level?

What attracted you to these fields of study?

Discipline/Profession

With what discipline and/or profession do you identify? For example, if you are a secondary school teacher, what subject do you teach—math, chemistry, history, language arts? These represent the discipline from which you are drawing. Similarly, if you are a school administrator, what theoretical fields do you draw from to understand the demands of your profession—e.g., organizational theory, leadership theory, economic theory, political theory, systems theory? If you teach in a professional school, what bodies of knowledge do you draw from—e.g., current developments in the profession, current pedagogical practices, curriculum theory?

If you have kept notes from your courses, review these. See if any ideas jump out at you. What was the source of the ideas?

Have you developed a personal library of books, articles, and other resources that matter to you? If so, which ones have influenced your thinking? Are any connected directly or indirectly to the troubling moments you have experienced?

 If you haven't created a professional library, start now. The issues that trouble you now are likely to resurface throughout the course of your professional life. Collecting resources that help you to think about these issues can save you time and effort in the future.

Discourse Communities

Within any discipline and profession, there are multiple subgroups who espouse different ways of thinking and talking about their field. In the field of special education, for example, recent theories have emerged to challenge the long-standing dominance of behavioral theories of learning. STEM initiatives have challenged old models of teaching science and math. The same is true in language arts and social studies. Often there are heated debates about the nature of complex practices like school administration and educational policy. Those who adhere to a particular perspective constitute a community of discourse.

What are major discourse communities within your field?

With which discourse communities in your field do you most strongly identify? What have they contributed to your understanding of troubles you have identified?

What authors are criticizing the thinking of those with whom you identify? To what extent have you considered their perspectives?

Informal Fields of Study

In addition to formal fields of study, you may have areas of interest that you pursue outside of academic programs. Someone who is passionate about music or photography might take classes to improve their skills. Someone who loves poetry or science fiction might join a writing group. These also provide possible ways of thinking about the world, our profession, and our practice.

Record any areas that you study, not to earn a degree, but to hone abilities or gain knowledge that are important to you.

Reflect on the conceptual skills and intellectual capacities you are gaining from these informal studies and how they might be shaping your thinking about troubling aspects of practice.

Continuing Education

In what ways do you stay abreast of new developments in your field?

Make a note of workshops, conferences, books, journal articles, podcasts, etc. that have contributed to your understanding of your field of practice and what is troubling to you.

Reflective Interlude

Review the information that you recorded about troubling moments of practice. Look for connections between your personal concerns and bodies of knowledge you have studied. If you completed the statement, "What I really want to understand is…," carefully consider how it relates to your field of study/practice. For example, consider the difference between the statements, "What I really want to understand is…

- …how to motivate my students to value calculus.

- …what happens if I shift from a pedagogy of instruction to a pedagogy of engagement when I teach calculus.

At first glance the two might appear to be a different wording of the same concern. Upon closer consideration, however, the first statement begins to situate the study in the field of psychology where motivation of learning has been studied at great length. The second statement begins to situate the study in education where engagement has been studied. The "object" of study is also different. In the first statement, "student motivation and value" is the focus with the implication that what the teacher does will result in changing others. In the second statement, the concept of "pedagogical engagement within a calculus class" is the focus; setting the stage for the teacher to explain what she has learned about her own pedagogical practice. While either statement would require greater refinement, the difference between the two statements illustrates the importance of thinking about the knowledge you can bring to bear on your study. Play around with different wordings to express what you really want to understand. Share the statements with others to see how they interpret your intentions. *Scenario 7.1* illustrates the evolution and refinement of a study through writing and getting feedback.

SCENARIO 7.1
REFINING A FOCUS FOR INQUIRY

COMMENTARY

This example, provided by art educator Pam Krakowski, illustrates how her practice context, her concerns, and her background knowledge evolved into a clearer and clearer vision for her inquiry—a narrative study of narrative pedagogy. This illustrates a process of "writing one's way into an inquiry." As Pam shared each version of her thinking with a dissertation study group, she used their feedback to sharpen the focus for her dissertation.

As you read through the following three charts, notice the overlap of ideas among the three drafts. A superficial reading could give the impression that Pam is merely reshuffling the same information, and to a certain extent, this is the case. Beyond that, however, each draft not only includes bits of new information, but also shows different relationships among recurring concepts—personal narrative, pedagogy, entering the child's world, and child-centered versus subject-centered art education.

MARCH DRAFT		
Working Title	Entering the child's world: A narrative study of young children's art making in an integrated art setting. OR Entering the child's world: A narrative study of an art teacher's adaptation of the Reggio Emilia approach. OR Toward a new paradigm: Finding the balance between child-centered and subject-centered approaches to teaching art.	In the first two titles, Pam is referring to "narrative" as a genre for her inquiry. Interestingly, the third title introduces the concept of "balance," but the focus is on balancing two different approaches to teaching art. This concept resurfaces in the August draft but with an important difference.
Intent of Study	To study my classroom to inform my pedagogy. (To find the most insightful, meaningful ways to teach art to young children.)	This intent has an outward focus on Pam's classroom, rather than an inward focus on her pedagogy. The two are obviously connected, but it matters what is put in the foreground and what is the background (context) of the study.
Context	I hope to study one of my early childhood, multi-age (K-1-2) art classes throughout the year. This would include once-a-week, 1-hour art classes; short- and long-term projects integrated with their home room teacher; small groups during and after school. This is a class where I have been collaborating with the classroom teacher in adapting the Reggio approach.	In addition to flagging her classroom as the context, Pam begins to imagine the types of information she can gather to fulfill the intent of her study. This is an example of disciplined (rather than casual) reflection. The proposed length of her information collecting and the variety of information illustrates the idea of "thick, rich" texts.

Importance of the Study	In the '50s and '60s, art education was dominated by a child-centered approach to the teaching of art which focused on the child, creativity and self-expression. During the 60s, with the influence of Sputnik and a return to basics, the pendulum began to swing to a more subject-centered approach to teaching art. The subject-centered approach, commonly known as discipline-based art education, focused on teaching the art contents or disciplines—studio production, aesthetics, art criticism, and art history. The leading researchers in these areas were theorists primarily working with adults. They influenced curriculum development, leaving out the importance of understanding child development and how young children think and learn. Currently, there is beginning to be a call for a balance between subject-centered and child-centered approaches. Note: I am not sure if child-centered is the word that I am looking for. I would certainly have to define it—but it also is a "loaded" word with a lot of negative connotations in art education, so maybe another word or phrase would be better. It also may be too narrow for what I want to cover.	This is a nice example of a concise description of different discourses within a field of study. In her final dissertation, this summary could be part of an introductory chapter. Pam elaborates on these different schools of thought about the teaching of art in her dissertation as a way of situating her own thinking within the field of art education. Notice Pam's final note where she expresses her misgivings about the term "child-centered." This is an example of sensitivity to language and how a concept can connote different meanings to different discourse communities.

APRIL DRAFT		
Working Title	Entering the child's world: A narrative study of studio art as pedagogy in early childhood.	In this draft, Pam has narrowed the options for her title, has eliminated the idea of "subject-centered" teaching of art, and has eliminated a focus on Reggio Emilia.
Intent of Study	To delineate (portray) studio art as pedagogy in early childhood. To examine the pedagogy of studio art in early childhood.	Notice how Pam is beginning to bring the idea of pedagogy into the foreground. She has also incorporated the concept of "early childhood" using it to replace "young children" that appeared in the title and intent of the March draft. This is significant because "early childhood" is a field of study with its own discourses. At this stage of her thinking, Pam has now begun to situate her study at the intersection of two fields of study—art education and early childhood education.

Pam had taken courses on early child development taught by a nationally recognized expert in the field (and subsequently a member of her committee). On her own, she had travelled to Italy to learn firsthand about the Reggio Emilia approach to teaching. Given this background knowledge, she could situate her study in the field of art education or early child development or the intersection of the two. This is an example of bringing one's existing knowledge to bear on an inquiry. |

Context	My K-3 students at the laboratory school. If needed, I could also include the 3 to 5-year olds at the museum.	In this draft she is still weighing options for the context of her study.
Importance of the Study	Children in the early childhood years present developmental and cognitive challenges vastly different from those of older children. How do we design art education programs for young children that have characteristics and patterns uniquely their own?	By adding a new first paragraph, Pam begins to lay a rationale for studying the intersection of art education and early childhood education. This is an example of a warrant that she develops more fully in her dissertation.
	In the 50s and 60s, a child-centered approach to art, emphasizing creativity and self-expression, dominated the field of art education. Over the last 20 years the emphasis has changed to a focus on the disciplines, or contents, of art education—studio production, aesthetics, art history, and art criticism. Each of these disciplines has pedagogical practices of its own. The theorists writing about these disciplines are often writing for adults or older children and have overlooked the importance of understanding the young child—how he/she thinks, learns, etc.—when designing curriculum. In my field there is a need to find a more child-centered approach to teaching the young child.	Consider whether Pam's description of her field has given you a brief, but clearer understanding, of art education discourses. This is an example of the educative nature of a Scholar-Practitioner Inquiry.

| My Back-ground

Interest | Seventeen years ago, I taught art to blind children. Many of my art classes were with children 3-8 years old. During those years, my pedagogy began to be defined, it was important to listen carefully to the children and to understand the world from their point of view.

After teaching at this school for 11 years, I left to take a job at a private school, teaching art to children, K-8. I found myself frustrated that I could not do many of the things I had done with the blind students. My class size was 24 instead of 4. I had no assistant. . . . The children were disruptive and much of my initial time was spent on classroom management.

After I had been teaching there for 5 years, I began to hear about the Reggio Emilia preschools. As I studied their philosophy and pedagogy, I discovered that many of my beliefs were consistent with theirs. I was inspired to understand and incorporate many of their principles in my own pedagogy. | The March draft did not include a personal background section. At that time, however, she did talk with her dissertation study group about her teaching experiences—usually referencing her time at the school for blind children. Often, she related quite lengthy anecdotes about the children and the lessons she taught; often the details were so overwhelming it was nearly impossible to see what issues might be studied. In the April draft, Pam began to incorporate these anecdotes into her writing. This began to create a stable text of her experiences which made it possible to look more carefully at the significant issues buried in the details.

This is a nice example of drawing upon knowledge from multiple experiences to inform one's thinking about a study. It also illustrates a commitment to deep learning as Pam pursued knowledge that addressed the dissonance (trouble) she was experiencing. |

AUGUST DRAFT		
Working Title	Although Pam kept the same title in the April and August drafts, she ultimately titled her dissertation *Balancing the Narrative and the Normative: Pedagogical Implications for Early Childhood Art Education*. Recall that the concept of "balance" appears in one version of her March titles. That concept continued to linger in the background, but emerged in Pam's final study—not as a balance between two different approaches to teaching art, but as a balance within her own pedagogy between her instructional goals for children (the normative) and learning that emerged by engagement with the children (the narrative).	
Intent of Study	To do a narrative study of my pedagogy, I would explore the use of narrative (as personal experience) in the teaching of art to children K-8 at a laboratory school.	Notice Pam has added another meaning to the concept of "narrative." In earlier drafts she used it to connote a genre of inquiry. Here she uses it to connote a mode of teaching (actually a philosophy of teaching that became clearer in her dissertation). This layering of meaning adds depth to Pam's study by aligning her mode of inquiry with her mode of teaching. Making the distinctions between these two uses of the concept clear in her dissertation called for skillful writing.
Context	Pam's title—Entering the child's world: A narrative study of studio art as pedagogy in early childhood—now reflects a shift in her thinking from a practice context to a conceptual context for her study. By situating her study in the field of early childhood education she gave herself leeway to draw upon her wealth of experience in a variety of settings to illustrate aspects of balancing the normative and narrative.	

| Importance of the Study | Rationale: Part of the "so what" of this study is that art teachers who are being trained with content-based curriculum models, often are not prepared to understand what is really meaningful to children in the art making process. They are taught to plan curriculum even before they meet the children and know their interests. Curriculum is often imposed upon the children instead of emerging from the children's developmental and personal interests and experiences. Listening to children, watching their play, hearing their stories, observing their art making, and taking note of their personal narrative themes in their art and play can assist the art teacher in planning curriculum and designing art experiences that are meaningful for the children. | This is an example of identifying potential audiences for the results of the study. It is also an example of a "claim" she is making—i.e., art teachers may lack an understanding of early child development. This will need to be warranted in the dissertation. |

| My Back- ground Interest | I've always been interested in the narrative quality of children's artwork. I've been interested in the stories that they tell and in the stories that they act out in their play. It seems that whatever art lessons I've done with children, I have always ended up tapping into their own personal narratives. Most often these lessons were based on the themes that I observed in their art making, storytelling, and play. To me, this has been the key to entering their worlds and finding out what was most meaningful to them. | Here Pam adds a third layer of meaning to "narrative," that of the children. In this statement of interest, she returns to the idea of "entering a child's world" and reveals its significance to her. Without this connection, it might seem like she was trying to have a clever title. Throughout the dissertation she offers examples of how she listens to the children's narratives. Through those experiential texts she warrants the idea of "entering the child's world" as an interpretive heuristic. It captures the essence of a narrative pedagogy that stands in tension with normative pedagogy. To convey this tension and the need for balance, Pam uses the mobiles of Alexander Calder as a visual metaphoric heuristic. |

Chapter 8

Situating My Thinking in a Broader Intellectual Landscape

*Where does my understanding fit
within my field(s) of practice?*

*Who else is thinking about
the issues that concern me?*

*What insights can they provide to
deepen and broaden my thinking?*

Purpose

As ideas for your inquiry continue to evolve, it is important to ask:

- Am I the only one who doesn't understand this problem/issue/ question?

- Have others provided insights that will alleviate my confusion or add to my knowledge?

- What aspects of this dilemma have been studied; what aspects have been overlooked?

- From what perspectives have my questions been studied?

- Do I have a perspective that has not been taken into account?

The purpose of the Exploratory Phase mentioned in Chapter 1 is to gather information that sheds light on these questions. Proposing a topic for inquiry that has been exhaustively studied can make you seem naïve. To avoid this pitfall, it is important to see how your thinking is connected (or disconnected) from the bodies of knowledge in your field of practice. By the end of the Exploratory Phase you should be able to articulate a clear statement of intent for your inquiry and a rationale for its importance. The intellectual work related to these prompts includes:

- weighing your ideas in light of the "experts'" ideas,
- weighing the credibility of the various "experts" within the field (e.g., whose ideas are taken seriously; whose tend to be dismissed), and
- identifying the discourse communities to which the authors belong.

 A good research librarian can be your best ally in finding relevant sources of information.

Reflective Prompts

Theoretical/Conceptual Frameworks or Analysis of Issues

Start with the work of authors with whom you are familiar. Have they written other materials that you should review?[1]

- Journal articles
- Books
- Conference Papers
- Workshops
- Ted Talks
- YouTube Videos

---

1   To avoid cumbersome, repetitive wording, we will often use "written" or "published" generally to refer to a variety of print and non-print media.

Review the bibliographies in books and articles to identify other scholars who are writing about the ideas you are exploring.

Statistics

Will you need statistics to show to what extent a situation exists or how many people are affected by the issue you are studying? Tap into existing data sources.

> *Federal and state* data bases often have useful statistics. For example, if you want to know the rate at which children from economically disadvantaged communities drop out of school, that data exists. If you want to know how many public, private, and charter schools exist or how many teachers work in each setting, these data exist.

> Many *professional organizations* also collect large scale data that can be tapped. For example, if you want to know how many nurse educators are prepared at a doctoral level and whether that doctorate is in nursing or education, it is likely that these data exist. If you want to know if membership in teacher unions has increased or decreased over the past decade, the various unions are likely to have that data.

> Given the proliferation of *organizational websites* hosted by groups with special interests, an Internet search is likely to provide additional sources of statistics. For example, if you are a teacher developing curriculum on the environment, the Old Growth Forest Network website provides statistics on the number of old growth forests remaining in the United States.

Research Findings

- Most often the results of research are reported in peer-reviewed, scholarly journals;
- Papers presented at scholarly conferences are often available by contacting the researcher;
- Dissertations/theses, dissertation abstracts

A Note on Social Media

The Internet has given us access to information that would have been unimaginable in the past. Obviously, all information on the web is not equal. Today, well respected scholars maintain blogs, do podcasts, and post lectures on YouTube. These are extremely valuable sources of the scholars' current thinking. At the same time, there are blogs maintained by highly opinionated but poorly informed individuals. In between are thousands of bloggers who offer insightful thoughts about their experiences, share their expertise, or comment on current affairs. Any or all of this information is potentially useful, depending on the intent of your Scholar-Practitioner Inquiry. What is absolutely essential is to understand what the information represents and to make that clear when you incorporate it into your study.

As you work on the Reflective Prompts, you are likely to find new resources that relate to potential avenues of study. Some of these may be sufficiently compelling to review immediately. Others you may want to add to your files to study more carefully at a later time.

Reflective Interlude

Keep working back and forth between resources you are finding, what you already know, and question(s) that you want to study. Keep in mind that you are looking not only for information that supports your hunches/opinions. You want to push to see if there are contrary points of view.

As you encounter perspectives that differ from yours, see if you can identify assumptions that underlie each perspective. As you identify your assumptions ask, "What is the source of this assumption? Why do I think this to be the case?" Unearthing and examining taken-for-granted assumptions are major aspects of Scholar-Practitioner Inquiry. This will also help you to shape an intent for your study that goes beyond confirming what you already think. It will take you to the edge of your knowledge, which is where inquiry begins.

Do not look only for authors who share the same points of view. That is useful, but finding divergent points of view is also extremely important. Particularly valuable are books that trace the development of ideas or journal articles that synthesize various schools of thought about a topic. Encyclopedias, handbooks, and compendia can be especially helpful in providing a wide range of views. (Look again at the *Scenario 7.1*. See how Pam mentions different schools of thought about how art should be taught to children. This is an example of how you begin to lay out different perspectives.)

Sometimes exploring existing bodies of knowledge can seem overwhelming. There is so much to read, so much to learn. One student wrote about this as the "Henny Penny Stage" of her inquiry (*Scenario 8.1*).

Working through the Exploratory Phase takes time and is not a linear process. Iterative cycles of reading, writing, and sharing your ideas will allow you to conceptualize a clear and cogent statement of intent for your inquiry.

Set up a system for keeping track of the sources of potentially useful information and also your notes about potential uses for the information. You don't want to run across a journal article sitting on your desk and wonder, "Why did I think this was so important? How did I imagine using it?"

....

SCENARIO 8.1
SITUATING YOUR THINKING
WITHIN BROADER DISCOURSES

COMMENTARY

Marjorie B. Logsdon went from a state of overwhelming confusion to a clearly focused study of pedagogical power and her struggle to transform her teaching practice. The following description captures the state of confusion often arising early in the Exploratory Phase. Giving oneself time to explore is crucial. Yet finding a way out of the confusion is also crucial. As Marjorie's musings on the turnpike illustrate, we become immersed in the ideas we are exploring. They surface in unexpected moments and often it's those moments that hold a key insight. When Marjorie comes to the concept of "authority," she finds the hook upon which to fasten the swirling array of ideas. As she resonated with that concept, she began to own her study. Marjorie claimed "personal essay" as her genre which was perfectly suited to her background as a teacher of literature and a strong creative writer. The conventions of personal essay also gave her the leeway to pursue ideas in a non-linear way which fit with her natural mode of thinking.

Her dissertation, written as a collection of essays, has been published as *A Pedagogy of Authority* (Pittsburgh: Learning Moments Press, 2017).

When I was in the Henny Penny stage of organizing this comprehensive exam question—you know, the frantic time of darting about screaming, "the sky is falling, the sky is falling"—I jumped from article to article in a frenetic clip, jotted down notes and fragments of ideas, wrote commands on the cover of texts that said, "Get this." I was in the evacuation mode of grabbing things to possess them. I was a mess. I made Henny Penny look catatonic. Then I'd talk to myself. "Slow down," I'd say. "Panicking will get you nowhere." Ok. Ok. I resolved. Begin at the beginning. Read a research proposal or a college text about feminist theory that will serve as a review for you; this will get you focused and maybe uncover a way to go that will be helpful. Satisfied that I at least had not yet been struck by catastrophe, I had found a place where I felt safe. Ok, I know this, I'd say as I read. Yes. I understand that. Then I would read the names of scholars seminal to the theory whom I hadn't read, or I'd read bibliographies, and the panic happened all over again. How could I have formed my topic last summer and not have read so and so? How could this one's work be so significant, and I hadn't even heard of her? "What a thrice triple ass am I," I'd say to myself as Caliban did; you don't know this, or you didn't read that. "Abusing myself to myself," I'd start darting about again, practically stopping people on the street to complain that I'd be on Medicare before I even wrote my comp, let alone the dissertation.

Then it hit me. Not the sky, but maybe a piece of it. I had tried to sort through the differing strands of feminism—the liberals, the radicals, the Marxists, the post-moderns, the socialist, the psychological—and make sense of them. I found strands of commonality in feminist pedagogy and discovered who thought what about what—or at least I was beginning to understand. I thought knowledge, gender, subjectivity, authority, the personal and emancipatory goals were all significant. But everything seemed to overlap. Some scholars had moved from Marxist feminism to postmodern feminism. Some authors declared themselves occupants of a few places—like critical theorist and educationalist—or were in no place or multiple places. Everything seemed to be moving and shifting (except me)—even the focus of major disciplines in feminism. I was quite overwhelmed in trying to understand it all. In fact, there was no way that I could understand it all.

Then, while driving on the turnpike, I started thinking once again about teaching and feminism, and I was trying to once again sort through what the scholars said, through what I knew, and what I felt I needed to know—talk about too much world and too little time. I just couldn't seem to narrow my focus to make all of this manageable. But finally, I asked myself what thing or things really bothered me about this teaching change of mine. I thought about the basketball story I had written and the story about W & J. I thought about my English classes and what I struggled with in the past two years. Authority. Authority and problems with what it means, how it is construed, sharing it, losing it, or not claiming it—these issues seemed to be the seat of real trouble for me. Why not think this thing, the comp, through myself? This might be a way "in," a way to come to grips with things that had eluded me. And it certainly seemed not only workable but feminist in approach. Perhaps this will work, I thought, so I began anew.

CHAPTER 9

Developing a
Game Plan for Study

What are the gaps in my understanding?

How do I want to address these gaps through my study?

What forms of information will I need to fulfill the intent of my study?

Purpose

Chapter 8 prompted you to look at where your thinking fits within a broader intellectual landscape. Through your reading and conversations, you should begin to identify gaps in your understanding of the issue(s) that trouble you. Those gaps point to possible avenues of inquiry. By crafting a statement of intent for your study, you identify the avenue you plan to pursue. Guiding questions outline a game plan for gathering information to fulfill the intent of the study. As you continue your explorations, begin to cluster information sources according to their usefulness in warranting various aspects of your study.

Reflective Prompts

What information sources help me to clarify the concepts I will use to describe my topic?

> Keep in mind that a dictionary definition is likely to be minimally useful. If your concept is important, there is likely to be a body of literature that discusses it. Use this literature to clarify the meaning of the term that is relevant to your inquiry.

> Do not look for a single, "correct" definition. Often the meaning of terms is debated by scholars within a field of study. Your role as an inquirer is to understand the various meanings and then explain how these meanings inform your thinking.

> It is possible that you may want to synthesize elements of multiple definitions to more accurately reflect your thinking about the term.

What information sources will help me to answer the question, "Why is this study important?"

> Often this question is stated in terms of "the significance of the study."

> Recall that in the Preface we said that the question you study has to matter to you. It also has to matter to your field of study and/or your profession.

> Perhaps the issue you want to study affects a large number of people. In such a case, statistics from a data base you have flagged will be used to demonstrate the relevance of your question.

> Perhaps your issue relates to a new policy initiative that impacts educational practice. Professional organizations may have issued a position statement

about the policy. These official positions can support your contention that the policy merits further study.

What information sources will help me explain what is already known about my issue?

Formal inquiries typically contain a review of literature which helps to set the boundaries of the study. The hypothetical examples in Scenario 3.1 illustrate different ways of framing an issue for study. Although those examples relate to case study, it is important to set the conceptual parameters—the *conceptual context*—of your study.

As you review the sources of information you've identified, look for multiple perspectives on your issue. This will be one way to eventually organize a review of literature.

Another potential way to organize literature sources is chronologically. Suppose, for example, you are interested in charter schools. You would want to trace the development of the charter school movement: when and where did it begin; who were its proponents and opponents; how many charter schools have been opened over a given time span; how many have closed; what are projections for the future of charter schools?

What information sources will give me greater insight into the issue(s) that trouble me?

As you scout for potentially useful sources of information, it is likely you will find books and articles written about your topic. Suppose, for example, you are interested in classroom management. Much has been written on the topic, and reading this body of literature can be part of your inquiry process.

If you want personal experiences or perspectives on an issue, have you found memoirs or blogs that can contribute to your inquiry?

What information sources will help me understand interpretive inquiry and my inquiry genre?

Reflective Interlude

As you sort through the information sources you have discovered, continue to refine the question(s) that you want to study. Some of your questions may have been so thoroughly studied that further inquiry is unnecessary. Others may become less interesting to you. Scratch those off your list. You may begin to see connections among previously separate questions and begin to synthesize those into a single overarching question.

Organize your information sources into two broad groupings—(1) those you need to consult as you prepare a proposal for your study, and (2) those you will consult as part of your inquiry process.

Keep in mind that you are likely to find additional sources of relevant information once you are immersed in your study. Continue to update your notes. Think of yourself as a detective following where the clues lead you.

CHAPTER 10

Claiming an Interpretive Inquiry Genre

What are my sources of knowledge about "research method"?

In what inquiry genre am I working?

What is my rationale for this genre?

How am I following the conventions of this genre?

Purpose

As discussed in Chapters 2-4, claiming an inquiry genre entails an understanding of your own proclivities for making meaning of experience. Understanding the assumptions you bring to the process will help to clarify your stance in relation to the topic of your study. As you become more familiar with the conventions of the genre you are claiming, the better prepared you will be to develop the logic-of-justification for each step of your study.

Margaret Mead once said, "If a fish were an anthropologist, the last thing it would discover would be water." Like fish, we grow up in a milieu that is so much a part of our reality that we tend not to notice it. Scholar-Practitioners often bring to their inquiries a set of taken-for-granted epistemological, ontological, and axiological assumptions that constitute their world view. Often, asking directly, "What's my world view?" isn't very helpful. Until we enter into a study, we may get only indirect glimpses of our world view. The following prompts suggest ways in which you can catch sight of the intellectual "water in which you are swimming."[1]

Reflective Prompts

When you think about doing scientific research, what adjectives come to mind?

When you think about doing an interpretive inquiry, what adjectives come to mind?

In what ways are the two lists of adjectives similar and different?

What is your understanding of interpretive inquiry as a tradition for generating knowledge?

What is the nature of knowledge you want to generate through your inquiry?

What research courses have you taken?

What have you learned about interpretive inquiry in these courses?

If you have not taken any research courses, what courses on interpretive inquiry are available at your university? [2]

What professors in your school or department understand interpretive inquiry and can guide your learning and your study?

What scholars in your field of study understand interpretive inquiry? Might they be willing to work with you?[3]

---

1 Often students ask if it is possible to change one's world view. A book edited by Heshusius and Ballard (1996) offers insightful accounts by noted researchers and evaluators of their transition from positivist to more interpretivist world views. Tananis (2000, 2006) coined the term "epistemorph" to describe her attempt at a metamorphosis from a positivist to interpretivist world view. (See also Piantanida, Tananis, & Grubs, 2004.) Full citations are in the bibliography.

2 The phrase "interpretive inquiry" may not appear in course titles. Sometimes "qualitative research" is used for alternatives to scientific (or quantitative) research courses. Many courses focus more narrowly on a particular method (e.g., action research) or technique (e.g., interviewing). Such courses can be very useful **IF** you understand how and why this information is relevant to **your** inquiry.

3 The Reflective Prompts in Chapter 12 ask you to consider institutional requirements for the dissertation. Often dissertation guidelines address the composition of your dissertation committee. See if you are expected to include a member from outside of your department or school. If so, consider what nationally recognized interpretive scholars might serve on your committee. The logistics of involving them in meaningful ways have become far more feasible

What books and articles have you read about interpretive inquiry? As you read books about your topic, are you particularly drawn to the way in which authors have investigated the topic they are discussing? How have they described their method? Do they cite others who have written about the method?

As you reflect on various sources of information, notice the language the authors use as well as their stance, voice, and tone. With which styles do you resonate?

What theses or dissertations have you read? Have you found any that might serve as an example to guide your own thinking?

What research experience(s) have you had in the past? Have you written research papers for courses or done an honors thesis as an undergraduate? Have you written a Master's thesis? Have you worked as a research assistant on someone else's project?

Reflective Interlude

Review the information you recorded for Chapter 7 about your disciplinary background. How does that background prepare you to work in a scientific tradition; in an interpretive tradition? To which tradition are you instinctively drawn? Did your course work better prepare you for scientific or interpretive forms of inquiry? (For example, if you teach science, you may be better prepared to design and conduct a scientific study. If you teach English literature, you may be better prepared to conduct an interpretive study.)

Review your notes in Chapter 6 about what troubles you. What types of questions did you generate? Do you want to prove the extent to which something is happening? Do you want to prove the efficacy of a particular instructional intervention? Are you trying to understand the nuances of a particular pedagogical challenge? How does the wording of your questions give hints of your world view?

Review your notes about your prospective audience(s). Do you understand the research/inquiry traditions that are seen as legitimate by these groups?

given increasingly sophisticated video conferencing technology.

What will you do if you see a mismatch between what you want to do and what your audience(s) value? Review *Scenario 2.2* for an example of this situation.

CHAPTER 11

Where Is My Inquiry Headed?

What do I intend to produce
as a result of my inquiry?

Who will find the results of my inquiry to be
useful?

Purpose

This chapter focuses on the end of your inquiry—not the substance but the form. The form will help you to decide how much information you will need to gather, what you will do with it, and how it will be presented. Consider, for example, the difference between conducting an inquiry to develop a policy, a course, or a dissertation. The following prompts invite you to consider what audience(s) will be interested in your inquiry results and the form those results will take. Although we begin with Prompts about the Master's Thesis and Dissertation, we flag a variety of formats that may be useful both to Scholar-Practitioners enrolled in formal academic programs and those who are not.

Reflective Prompts

Format

Are you working on a Master's thesis, doctoral dissertation, or some other form of capstone scholarly project?

Are you developing curriculum for a course or workshop?
Are you trying to formulate a policy?
Are you planning to write a book or journal article?
Are you planning to write a grant proposal?
Are you planning to produce a video?
Are you preparing a presentation for a professional conference?
Have you decided to start a blog?
What other format(s) might you have in mind?

Audience

If you are working on a Master's thesis, dissertation, or capstone project to what discourse(s) will your inquiry contribute?[1]

What group(s) will be reading the book or journal article you write?

If you are developing a curriculum, what is the age and background of the students? What instructional materials and modalities will you be developing?

What group will be reviewing and accepting (or rejecting) your policy or your grant proposal—a school district, a national professional association, a committee, a philanthropic foundation?

Do you intend to use your video with students, other professionals, or a broader general audience?

As you brainstorm about potential audiences for your work, ask yourself:

- Who needs to know what I'm finding out?
- Why would they care?
- What would be useful to them?
- Where do they typically turn for information needs?

---

1 A longstanding stereotype has been that theses and dissertations sit on library shelves (or digital files) never to see the light of day. This would truly be a sad result from all the effort you've invested in your study. It would mean that you gave insufficient attention to the "So What" question.

Reflective Interlude

As you imagine the final outcome of your inquiry, review the notes you have been making about various types and sources of information you are gathering. Do you have what you need? Are there gaps you still need to fill? Continue to refine your game plan if you are still developing a proposal. If you are working on the final report of your inquiry, continue to refine how you are using information sources to warrant your outcomes.

 A well-warranted conclusion typically comprises several lines of reasoning. You are likely to need different sets of information to develop and support each line of reasoning. Crafting a guiding question for each line of reasoning can help you organize the information you are accumulating. This also helps to explain the structure of your inquiry and your final product. Review Scenarios 3.4, 4.2, 4.3, and 6.2 for examples of guiding questions and how they lead to the structure of a dissertation.

CHAPTER 12

Balancing Creativity with External Requirements

What institutional requirements am I expected to meet?

Purpose

Throughout the book we have mentioned that interpretive inquiry is embedded in the knowledge traditions of the arts and humanities. We have alluded to the creativity involved in interpreting and portraying insights gained through your inquiry. In this chapter, we look at some practicalities that you may need to consider in order to meet organizational requirements.

Reflective Prompts

Thesis, Dissertation, or Capstone Project

What are your institution's requirements for the thesis, dissertation, or capstone project?

Have you discussed these requirements with your thesis/dissertation advisor?

How much leeway or flexibility will you have in shaping your study?

What formatting guidelines are you expected to follow?

What are the procedures for electronic submissions?

Will your study have to be reviewed and approved by your institution's Ethics Committee (often called an Institutional Review Board)? Have you taken this review process into account when you projected a timeline for graduation?

If your inquiry will be situated in a particular institution, what permissions will you need to gain access?

Books and Journal Articles

If you are planning to publish your inquiry results in the form of a book, what publishers are you considering? What are their submission procedures (e.g., do they want a query letter, must you work through an agent, how do you contact their acquisition editor)?

If you are planning to publish journal articles, review the submission guidelines that are typically found on the editorial page. Or visit the journal's website to see what guidelines are provided. If you're not sure whether your article(s) will meet the guidelines, follow up with an email or phone call.

A useful strategy for pursuing this information is to visit book and journal exhibits at professional conferences. Typically, publishing companies will have an editor attend these conferences. Find publishers whose books or journals have subjects and audience that are similar to the book or article you plan to write.

Also, publishers are interested in knowing the audience for your proposed work. If you have a blog with a substantial number of followers, that may strengthen your proposal.

Conference Presentations

Often professional associations put out calls for conference papers through their journal, newsletter, or website. Keep an eye on the associations you are interested in. Note the time frame for submitting a proposal and whether you have to submit the completed presentation prior to the conference.

Pay particular attention to the length of submissions and any special formatting requirement.

Consider various presentation formats (e.g., paper presentation by single author, panel, roundtable, or poster session). As you proceed through your inquiry, you may be able to make use of different formats. For example, as you are beginning to conceptualize your conclusions, you might do a poster presentation that will help you better to understand your audience or to recognize where greater clarity is needed. If you have identified a discourse community that you want to join, consider inviting members of that community to serve on a panel with you— even if early on you feel comfortable only in the role of moderator.

Policy Recommendations

To what organizations would these recommendations be submitted? In what format should the policy be presented? What process does the organization expect you to follow when making a recommendation? Who has the authority to accept and approve your recommendations?

Course or Workshop

Under what auspices would a course or workshop be offered? What procedures are you expected to follow in proposing a course or workshop? What format are you expected to follow?

Grant Proposals

There are several national databases that provide information on potential sources of grant funding. These can be searched by topic area, geographic region, funding priorities, typical amount funded, etc. As you identify possible funding sources, pay close attention to their funding guidelines and submission procedures. Note funding cycles and eligibility requirements.

Blogs

Blogs can range in format from fairly informal to very polished. What do you have in mind?

Podcasts

A number of good references provide useful information about starting a podcast. How long should it be? What format will you use (e.g., conversation or interviews; single host or co-hosts)? What technology will you need?

Videos

If you are planning to air your videos through avenues like YouTube, what guidelines will you need to follow?

Reflective Interlude

As you reflect on notes about your study, recognize the importance of balancing your own creative vision for your inquiry and any requirements you may be expected to meet. If the requirements seem to be too limiting, explore where you can push the boundaries, think flexibly, and talk with your advisor (or publisher or funder). Often there is more leeway than initially seems possible. Recognize, however, the more you deviate from accepted conventions, the clearer your logic-of-justification must be.

Review the information in all the previous chapters and try to write a one paragraph summary of what you want to study, why you want to study, who your intended audience is, and what format will you use to present your inquiry. Initially, this is likely to be rough. Continue to refine and polish it as you continue your exploration.

CHAPTER 13

From Moment to Meaning

*How will I use the information I've
gathered through my inquiry?*

Purpose

The prompts in Chapter 8 encouraged you to explore information sources that would help you to see how your thinking fits within a larger intellectual landscape. The prompts in Chapter 9 encouraged you to develop a game plan for gathering information needed to fill in the gaps. This chapter focuses on what you do with the information you have gathered. Making meaning of the information is the art of Scholar-Practitioner Inquiry. Because it is an art, no specific steps define the process. Therefore, in this chapter we offer some suggestions for how to think about the meaning-making process.

The first point we want to emphasize is the iterative and recursive nature of the process. You do not wait until all the information is gathered and then try to figure out what it means. You will constantly be assessing and reassessing how the accumulating information provides insight into the intent of your study and the guiding inquiry questions. As new potential sources of information come to light, you'll be tracking those down. You will be speculating, trying out interpretations, getting feedback on tentative outcomes. You'll be sifting and sorting—what is central, what is peripheral; what is in the foreground, what recedes into the background or disappears entirely.

The second point to keep in mind is the moment that started your inquiry. That is the foundation for your meaning-making process. By recalling that moment, you can begin to chart your path through the inquiry—how the moment led to a question; how the question led to an investigation; and how the investigation has led to conceptualization. How many details about this journey you share will depend on what outcome you will be presenting. Far fewer details will be needed for a policy recommendation than a thesis or dissertation. How you choose to lay out the details is part of the art of Scholar-Practitioner Inquiry.

When offering distinctions between scientific research and Scholar-Practitioner Inquiry, we suggested that "text" was a more useful term than "data." We use the term "Interpretive Text" as a descriptor for your final conceptualization of your inquiry. It portrays why you undertook the study; what you studied; your process of inquiry; and the meanings you have come to. An element of interpretation is inherent throughout the inquiry, but the Interpretive Text pulls all the pieces together into a final, comprehensive picture. The Interpretive Text is conceptualized as you draw from Experiential Texts and Discursive Texts to warrant multiple lines of reasoning.

Reflective Prompts

Experiential Texts

Experiential texts refer to accounts of experience which may be characterized as:

> Recollective accounts which describe situational details of an experience,

> Introspective accounts which express reactions to an experience, and/or

> Conceptual accounts which express an interpretation or meaning of an experience.

To illustrate the difference, imagine some friends show you the picture of a church they visited on their trip to Italy. One gives a recollective account saying, "Here's a church we visited on the first day of our trip." Another gives an introspective account saying, "Walking into this church filled me with awe." The third gives a conceptual account saying, "Walking into this church where the bones of martyrs are consecrated filled me with awe at the sacrifices people are willing to make for their beliefs. I'm not sure I'd be that courageous." Can you see how the third account incorporates details, feeling, and meaning? Experiential texts you gather (including those you generate about your own experience) can exhibit any or all of these reflective qualities. The intellectual work of a Scholar-Practitioner Inquiry entails interpreting what individual experiential texts mean in relation to the intent of your study. As you sort and sift the information you are gathering, consider the following forms and sources of experiential text. Keep in mind the following clusters are not exhaustive or mutually exclusive.

Experiential Texts—Capturing and Portraying Moments

Accounts of Personal Experience

- Interviews you conduct with others
- Observations of your own experiences as recorded in logs/journals/etc.
- Blogs
- Memoirs
- Anecdotes, your own and those from others

Artifacts of Experience

- Instructional plans and materials
- Student work
- Professional journal/log
- Videos

Opinions

- Editorials
- Blogs
- Position papers

Discursive Texts—Bridging from Moments to Meaning

As the name suggests, discursive texts are embedded in the on-going, evolving discourses in a field of study. The secondary sources you read during the Exploratory Phase are examples of discursive texts. Discursive texts can provide support for your interpretations of experiential texts. They also provide contexts for key concepts and warrants for particular perspectives. Keep in mind that you are likely to be weaving discursive texts throughout your study; they are not confined to a single chapter or a single review of literature. In one place you might be constructing a discursive text related to the intent of your study. In another place you might be constructing a discursive text related to your genre.

Existing Research & Theoretical Literature

- Articles
- Books
- Dissertations
- Conference presentations

Legal/Regulatory/Policy

- Congressional record
- Pending or enacted legislation

- Organizational archives (e.g., policy manuals, minutes of board meetings)
- Historical documents/archives

Emerging/Current/Cutting Edge Issues

- News media
- Hashtag movements
- Conference agenda/themes and presentations
- Implications for further study in research reports

Interpretive Text—Portraying Meaning

Interpretive Text ties all of the pieces of an inquiry together. It puts into perspective the conclusions you have reached and the thinking that led to those conclusions. This entails movement from the specific details of idiosyncratic experience to conceptual frameworks that portray meaning. Within some discourse communities these conceptual portrayals are considered theoretical constructs. Shawn Otto would disagree, stating:

> Scientists will tell us that much of the conceptual problem lies in the public's misunderstanding of the word "theory." A scientific theory is not a hypothesis or guess, as the word commonly means when used in casual conversation. A scientific theory is the one explanation that is confirmed by all the known and validated experiments performed to date...A theory is thus among the most certain forms of scientific knowledge...[1]

Otto is contrasting the meaning of formal scientific theory with the casual dismissal of ideas with the often self-serving phrase, "that's

---

1   Otto, 217-218.

just a theory." Otto who is himself constructing a rhetorical argument (i.e., there is a "war on science") might concede that scholarly, if not scientifically validated, theories are of value. We mention this issue to underscore the importance of understanding the nature of knowledge claims that can be supported through Scholar-Practitioner Inquiry.

Pat's portrayal of her narrative study (*Scenario 4.2*) offers a conceptual framework to portray four different ways in which students came to terms with the ambiguous task of portfolio-making: Searching for Boundaries, Finding a Voice, Pursuing Connections, Making Discoveries. These portrayals have not been validated by hundreds of experimental studies. Nor would it be particularly worthwhile to run experimental tests to see if they hold true across educational contexts. They do, however, give more nuanced ways of understanding students' learning and might serve as a counterpoint to simplistic rubrics to evaluate reflection.

In his book, *Teaching and Its Predicaments*, educator David Cohen makes a distinction between informal, ordinary instruction and the practice of teaching, saying:

> Teaching practice includes conscious efforts to make connections with learning in order to advance it. Wherever practicing teachers work and however fleetingly, they try to bridge the chasms that often yawn between teaching and learning. Deliberately seeking to make such connections is a crucial and even constitutive feature of teaching practice, and it depends among many other things, on the mutual mind reading that socio-biologists and anthropologists argue was essential to the evolution of our species. If teachers cannot somehow improve learning over what would occur in conventional, informal, or casual instruction, it is difficult to see what claim they might have to cultivate a practice of instruction.[2]

---

2   David K. Cohen. *Teaching and Its Predicaments* (Cambridge, MA: Harvard University Press, 2011), 33.

Cultivating a practice of instruction, Cohen contends, involves attention to what he characterizes as three terrains: (1) the knowledge that teachers extend to learners, and how they extend it; (2) the organization of instructional discourse; (3) teachers' acquaintance with students' knowledge.[3]

In talking about her struggles to make sense of 65 portfolios, Pat acknowledges her preconceptions about what student reflection would or should look like. If she held fast to those preconceptions, she could easily have dismissed the students' work as "non-reflective" and deemed them to be unsophisticated learners. Through her inquiry, however, she became deeply acquainted with her students' knowledge as well as their process for internalizing that knowledge. This kind of nuanced understanding is glossed over in what educator Helen Hazi calls "metrics mania"[4]—an obsession with objective, standardized measurement. By offering a heuristic representation of her insights, Pat offers other educators a new lens for understanding the nature of student reflection. We consider this a theoretic construct.

There are no specific procedures or protocols that lead to the creation of the Interpretive Text. In the end, it is the Scholar-Practitioners' sensibilities that allow for a conceptual leap from their original defining moment to meaning. Just as artists are the instruments through which art is created, Scholar-Practitioners are the instruments through which heuristic theoretical constructs are created. We hope the six scenarios provided in this chapter spark your understanding of what it means to claim your authority to imagine the results of your inquiry.[5]

Reflective Interlude

As you begin to identify sources of information, ask yourself:

- What does this information represent (e.g., someone's experience, someone's opinion, the results of a research project, a theoretical argument, a conceptual perspective)?

---

3 Cohn, 34.
4 Helen M. Hazi, *Metrics Mania*, retrievable from scholarpractitionernexus.com.
5 Noreen B. Garman and Maria Piantanida, *The Authority to Imagine: The Struggle toward Representation in Dissertation Writing* (full citation in bibliography). This edited book contains accounts written by the authors of the dissertations mentioned throughout *From Moment to Meaning*. Each account elaborates on how the author came to conceptualize the portrayal of her inquiry.

- How much credence can I place in this information (e.g., is it from a credible source; how was the information generated)?
- To what aspect of my study will this information contribute?
    * Does it support my contention that my problem is also a problem for a group of people like me?
    * Can I use it to clarify what I mean by a particular concept?
    * Does it offer a set of ideas I can build upon?
    * Does it offer contrasting points of view allowing me to demonstrate that I have thought of all sides of a problem?

As you review the scenarios, notice how the overarching framework for the portrayal of results does not lie in the individual experiential or discursive texts. The inspiration for constructing the overarching interpretive text often comes from outside the study per se. Notice, for example, how Pam and Wendy draw from their broader background in art for metaphors to structure their results. This is one reason we encourage you to think broadly about the knowledge you bring to your inquiry. The final scenario comes from Maria's dissertation and serves to illustrate the creative leap that occurs in interpretive inquiry.

SCENARIO 13.1
PORTRAYING THE PROBLEMATICS
OF EDUCATIONAL INCLUSION

We discussed Micheline Stabile's dissertation, *Problematizing Educational Inclusion*, in *Scenarios 1.3 and 4.3*. In this scenario we give a flavor of her heuristic portrayal. In Chapters 3 – 7, Micheline offered five different orientations toward educational inclusion.

- Politically-Oriented Images of Educational Inclusion
- Community-Oriented Images of Educational Inclusion
- Culturally-Oriented Images of Educational Inclusion
- Practically-Oriented Images of Educational Inclusion
- Moral/Ethical Images of Educational Inclusion

Each of these orientations was supported by vignettes she crafted from multiple experiential texts. In "Chapter 8—Understanding Educational Inclusion: From the Language of Technique to a Discourse of Ethics," she elaborates on the ethical dimensions of educational inclusion and bridges into her final heuristic, "The Callings of Conscience." With this as the umbrella concept, she then lays out the nature of the call for the first four orientations.

Political Images: The Call of Sacrifice

Community Images: The Call of Membership

Cultural Images: The Call of Memory

Practical Images: The Call of Craft

Her final chapter focuses on "The Call of Imagination," explicating a rationale for imagination as a means for recognizing "policies of inclusion—not as an imposition but as a possibility."

SCENARIO 13.2
PORTRAYING THE ART CLASSROOM

As you may recall from *Scenario 7.2*, art educator Pam Krakowski used the metaphor of Alexander Calder's mobiles to convey the tensions between normative and narrative pedagogies. You may also remember that she was torn between various schools of thought about how art should be taught to children and in what context she should embed her study. By the time she completed her inquiry, she had resolved these issues and created five chapters, each of which conceptualized the classroom as a different kind of space:

- Art Classroom as Museum Gallery
- Art Classroom as Studio
- Art Classroom as Haven
- Art Classroom as Stage
- Art Classroom as Laboratory

Pam concluded each chapter with a subsection titled "Balancing Lessons," in which she discussed issues of balancing the normative and the narrative.

SCENARIO 13.3
PORTRAYING REFLECTIVE ARTMAKING

Art educator Wendy Milne, whom we introduced in *Scenario 6.1*, also used an art-oriented metaphor to conceptualize her study. She portrays her dissertation as a one-woman exhibit for which she is both artist and docent. As she walks readers through each room of the gallery, she explains the significance of the included portraits. The following explanation introduced her logic-of-justification for the metaphor of portraiture.

"In order to enter into this next phase of reflective artmaking and to continue in an arts-based modality, I decided to create "portraits" from select artifacts generated during the initial seven weeks [of the study]. These portraits highlight insights I came to about reflection, artmaking, and pedagogy and are exhibited in Chapters 4 through 7. It is through the creation and exhibition of these portraits that I came to "conceptual reflection"... The purpose of this section [of the dissertation] is to explain how and why I created nine portraits for a one woman exhibit. To do so, I enter into the discourses related to portraiture. I then explain the procedures utilized to develop and exhibit all of the portraits. The portraits are:

- Portraits of Teacher as Reflective Artmaker
- Portraits of Teacher as Subject-Centered
- Portraits of Teacher as Artmaker
- Portraits of Teacher as Listener"

SCENARIO 13.4
PORTRAYING A LEAD TEACHER INITIATIVE

In *Scenario 3.4*, we mentioned Kathleen Ceroni's use of the term "inner views storied" as an example of a logic-of-justification. This concept became the conceptual frame for two chapters in her dissertation. In the first, she portrays the inner views:

- Grace's Story—The Dutiful Lead Teacher
- Sarah's Story—The Disillusioned Former Lead Teacher
- Mary Jane's Story—The Outspoken Leader Teacher Trainer
- Debbie's Story—The Cynical Non-Lead Teacher
- Ann's Story—The Detached Non-Lead Teacher
- Maggie's Story—The Acquiescent Lead Teacher
- Sue and Kate's Story—The Hopeful Lead Teachers

In the subsequent chapter, following the conventions of literary criticism, she interprets the stories for surface and embedded meanings to illuminate a range of responses to the Lead Teacher Initiative.

....

SCENARIO 13.5
PORTRAYING SPIRITUAL
INQUIRY & PEDAGOGY

In *Scenario 3.5*, we discussed Marilyn Llewellyn's logic-of-justification for a genre she named "spiritual inquiry." Her final Interpretive Text portrayed issues in the form of meditations:

- Meditation #1: Fractures, Awakenings, Bitter Wisdom and Conversion
- Meditation #2: Faith—Belief and Unseen Reality
- Meditation #3: Beyond Caring to Compassion
- Mediation #4: Revelation—Curriculum in Process
- Meditation #5: The Divine Wisdom of Lived Experience
- Meditation #6: Sacred Spaces

When she reworked her Project Demonstrating Excellence (her university's equivalent of a dissertation) as a book, she used the concept of "contemplation" as the organizing image for her Interpretive Text:

- Chapter 1: Contemplation on Pedagogy
- Chapter 2: Contemplation on Spirituality
- Chapter 3: Contemplation on Faith in Classroom Relationships
- Chapter 4: Contemplation on Praxis as Compassion
- Chapter 5: Contemplation as Revelation—Curriculum in Process
- Chapter 6: Contemplation on Being and Learning Together

Her book, *Spirituality and Pedagogy: Being and Learning in Sacred Spaces* is available through amazon.com.

....

SCENARIO 13.6
PORTRAYING A CONCEPTUAL LEAP

This passage comes from Maria's chapter on grounded theory. It is her "logic" for moving from specific data to a conceptual "so what." Her use of the term "data" is indicative of the time she was writing, when the notion of "text" had not been well articulated in the discourses of educational research.

"During one phase of my research, I carried with me a binder containing transcripts and coded data. When asked how my project was going, I would point to the binder and respond, 'Well, I have all this—this stuff—I've been gathering.' I was hard put to explain what I was researching and the nature of my results. One evening I was meeting with several other doctoral students, all of whom were conducting naturalistic [read interpretive] research projects. We met regularly as a study group to deal with methodological issues and that particular evening another member of the group was struggling to decide how to manage her reams of thick data. As she talked, I had the image of gathering colorful pebbles from a variety of beaches and then fussing endlessly to sort the pebbles into piles of comparable size, color, texture, beach of origin, etc. Despite the volumes of pebbles I had gathered, it seemed terribly superficial and banal to talk about the various piles. Slowly, I began to realize that I could use the pebbles in a very different way. I could stop trying to maintain the identity of each separate pebble, and could, instead, use them collectively to create a colorful mosaic. Suddenly, I realized that the significance of my data did not lie in the individual pieces of data, but rather in using the pieces to create a meaningful picture of hospital-based education...It is the researcher's theoretical sensitivity that allows for the movement from a collection of pebbles to a mosaic—from data to theory. And that sensitivity is the result of the researcher's knowledge, experience, intuition, and capacity for conceptualization."

Epilogue

EMBRACING A MINDSET OF SCHOLAR-PRACTITIONER INQUIRY

In closing, we return to our premise that Scholar-Practitioner Inquiries often begin when a troubling moment stirs a need for deeper understanding. The potential for transforming such troubling moments into meaningful insights hinges upon three questions:

- What can I learn by studying this experience?
- What is my responsibility to share my learning with others?
- Through what avenues can I share my learning?

By drawing upon the Scholar-Practitioner quality of Metacognitive Reflection, educators can craft stories of their experiences to provide deeper insights into the nuances of educational practice. During the COVID-19 pandemic, for example, a number of educators (including us) began to ask others to share their experiences with distance education. When the pandemic hit in the middle of the 2019-2020 school year, everyone was caught off guard. While some individuals and districts were better prepared to respond to the need for distance instruction, others struggled. Just getting through the year at a personal and professional level demanded enormous time and energy. Conducting a Scholar-Practitioner Inquiry was unlikely to be at the top of anyone's to do list. Yet, as the school year drew to a close, those with a Scholar-Practitioner mindset recognized the importance of gathering lessons learned, and took action.

The Scholar-Practitioner quality of Ethical Stewardship comes into play as educational practitioners take responsibility for learning from troubling moments. In our book, *On Being a Scholar-Practitioner*, we discuss three dimensions of stewardship—ethical conduct, advocacy, and commitment to inquiry. The many acts of caring during the pandemic exemplify stewardship as "ethical conduct"—from teachers who spent hours searching for resources to enhance distance learning for their students to school administrators who personally delivered diplomas—professionals responded creatively to fulfill their responsibilities.

Stewardship as advocacy and commitment to inquiry calls upon Scholar-Practitioners to share new-found knowledge with the broader field of education. Doing so draws upon the Scholar-Practitioner quality of Contextual Literacy. Educational practice occurs within nested contexts from the micro-level of classrooms to the macro-level of social movements. The boundaries between these contexts are porous, allowing knowledge to flow in multiple directions. Contextual Literacy allows Scholar-Practitioners to seek out and use channels of communication through which their knowledge can be shared. This, too, is part of Ethical Stewardship.

In recent years, researchers seeking strategies to improve the quality of education have recognized the limitations of studying classrooms (or even districts) as isolated entities. Acknowledging that education occurs within complex, overlapping systems, the Carnegie Foundation (a long-time driving force for educational reform) is encouraging the formation of networked improvement communities through which knowledge from multiple sources can be shared. These represent potential forums that Scholar-Practitioners might use to share the lessons learned. If opportunities to participate in a networked improvement community are unavailable in particular geographic areas, Scholar-Practitioners, as stewards of the profession, can draw upon their Contextual Literacy to create communities of practice where shared learnings can be accumulated.

Finally, the Scholar-Practitioner quality of Aesthetic Imagination can play a vital role in educational improvement initiatives. By imagination, we do not mean wishful or magical thinking. We share curriculum scholar Maxine Greene's view that imagination allows us "to see beyond what is to what might be."[1] For decades, reform initiatives have aimed at improving education within long-standing institutional structures. In January 2020, it was "unthinkable" that all education—from pre-K through graduate school—would shift to on-line instruction. Had educational reformers suggested such "an experiment," the outcry (both for and against) would have been deafening. However, by disrupting the routines, structures, and processes of education, the COVID-19 pandemic has created an unprecedented opportunity to re-imagine new systems of education.

From the micro-context of classrooms to the macro-context of education as a social institution, opportunities to envision a "new normal" abound. New visions of educational administration will be needed if the locus of schooling becomes bifurcated, sometimes occurring within school buildings and other times at home. Classroom scheduling and management concerns may become irrelevant. New policies and procedures may be needed for hiring, compensating, and supervising personnel. Support services—everything from cafeterias to transportation to building maintenance—will come under scrutiny. Centuries-long rituals that have shaped the culture of schooling may need to be replaced with rituals that create on-line communities.

The challenge facing everyone—teachers, administrators, school boards, policy makers, reform advocates, parents, government officials, educational researchers—is whether we will try to patch together the old structures, processes, and practices of education or imagine new, more vibrant systems. Can we structure into the "new normal" on-going forums for deep learning and generative deliberations among all those with a stake in the quality and equity of our nation's schooling? Will educational practitioners be seen, not as subjects to be improved through externally imposed reform initiatives, but as vital contributors to systemic reform?

Over the years, we have been privileged to work with the educators whose scholarly work is incorporated into this book. Our thinking has been enriched beyond measure by countless other colleagues who generously shared their knowledge. Beyond these colleagues, we

---

1 Maxine Greene, *Releasing the Imagination: Essays on Education, the Arts, and Social Change* (San Francisco: Jossey-Bass, 1995).

have been inspired by the many students who have demonstrated a commitment to deep learning—their own and their students'. Through formal and informal inquiries, all of these individuals have generated the type of practical wisdom so desperately needed in this time of disruption. As members of multiple communities of practice, we have seen how the qualities of pedagogical wisdom, theoretic understanding, contextual literacy, ethical stewardship, metacognitive reflection, and aesthetic imagination have nurtured a mindset for the art of practice and the art of Scholar-Practitioner Inquiry.

Bibliography

Bryk, Anthony S. "2014 AERA Distinguished Lecture: Accelerating How We Learn to Improve." *Educational Researcher* 44, 9 (2015); 467-477.

Bullock, A., O. Stallybrass, and S. Trmobley, eds. *The Fontana Dictionary of Modern Thought*, 2nd ed. London: Fontana, 1988.

Cohen, David K. *Teaching and Its Predicaments*. Cambridge, MA: Harvard University Press, 2011.

Flyvbjerg, Bent. *Making Social Science Matter: Why Social Inquiry Fails and How It Can Succeed Again*, trans. Steven Sampson. New York: Cambridge University Press, 2001.

Fowler, James W. *Stages of Faith: The Psychology of Human Development and the Quest for Meaning*. San Francisco: Harper & Row, 1981.

Garman, Noreen B. and Maria Piantanida, eds. *The Authority to Imagine: The Struggle toward Representation in Dissertation Writing*. Pittsburgh: Learning Moments Press, 2018.

Hammond, Linda Darling and Jeannie Oakes. *Preparing Teachers for Deeper Learning*. San Francisco: John Wiley & Sons, 2005.

Hazi, Helen M. *Metrics Mania*, retrievable from scholarpractitionernexus.com (S-P Library/Articles).

Kilbourn, Brent, "Fictional Theses in Educational Researcher," *Educational Researcher* 28, no 12 (1999): 27-32.

Kim, Suki. *Without You, There is No Us: Undercover among the Sons of North Korea's Elite*. New York: Penguin Random House, 2014.

McMahon, Patricia L. "From Angst to Story to Research Text: The Role of Arts-based Educational Research in Teacher Inquiry," *Journal of Curriculum Theorizing* 16, no1 (2000): 125-145.

Nash, Robert. *Liberating Scholarly Writing: The Power of Personal Narrative*. New York: College Teachers Press, 2004.

Otto, Shawn Lawrence Otto. *The War on Science: Who's Making It; Why It Matters; What We Can Do about It.* Minneapolis: Milkweed Editions, 2016.

Piantanida, M., Patricia L. McMahon, and Marilyn Llewellyn. *On Being a Scholar-Practitioner: Practice Wisdom in Action. Pittsburgh*: Learning Moments Press, 2019.

Pinar, William F., William M. Reynolds, Patrick Slattery, and Peter M. Taubman. *Understanding Curriculum*. New York: Peter Lang, 1995.

Smith, John K. and Lous Heshusius, "Closing Down the Conversation: The End of the Quantitative-Qualitative Debate among Educational Inquirers," Educational Researcher (January 1986): 4-12.

Sweet, Victoria. *Slow Medicine: The Way to Healing*. New York: Riverhead Books, 2017.

Ramo, Joshua Cooper. *The Age of the Unthinkable: Why the New World Disorder Constantly Surprises Us*. New York: Back Bay Books, 2009.

Ravitch, Diane. *Slaying Goliath: Passionate Resistance to Privatization and the Fight to Save America's Public Schools*. New York: Alfred A. Knopf, 2020.

Richardson, Laurel. *Writing Strategies: Reaching Diverse Audiences*. Qualitative Research Methods Series 21. Newbury Park, CA: Sage, 1990.

Schwartz, Barry and Kenneth Sharpe. *Practical Wisdom: The Right Way to Do the Right Thing*. New York: Riverhead Books, 2010.

Taleb, Nassim Nicholas. *Antifragile: Things that Gain from Disorder*. New York: Random House, 2012.

Learning Moments Press is a small, independent publishing company dedicated to sharing the wisdom that comes from thoughtful reflection on experience. The Wisdom of Practice Series showcases the work of individuals who illuminate the complexities of practice as they strive to fulfill the purpose of their profession.

Cooligraphy artist Daniel Nie created the logo for Learning Moments Press by combining two symbol systems. Following the principles of ancient Asian symbolism, Daniel framed the logo with the initials of Learning Moments Press. Within this frame, he has replicated the Adinkra symbol for *Sankofa* as interpreted by graphic artists at the Documents and Designs Company. As explained by Wikipedia, Adinkra is a writing system of the Akan culture of West Africa. *Sankofa* symbolizes taking from the past what is good and bringing it into the present in order to make positive progress through the benevolent use of knowledge. Inherent in this philosophy is the belief that the past illuminates the present and that the search for knowledge is a life-long process.